SEARCH FOR THE NILE'S SOURCE

John Petherick F.R.G.S.
H.M. consul for Soudan

SEARCH
for the
NILE'S SOURCE

THE RUINED REPUTATION OF JOHN PETHERICK,
NINETEENTH-CENTURY WELSH EXPLORER

John Humphries

UNIVERSITY OF WALES PRESS
CARDIFF
2013

www.uwp.co.uk

British Library Cataloguing-in-Publication Data
A catalogue record for this book is available from the British Library.

ISBN 978-0-7083-2673-2
e-ISBN 978-0-7083-2678-7

The publisher acknowledges the financial support of the Welsh Books Council.

Typeset by Chris Bell, cbdesign
Printed by CPI Antony Rowe, Chippenham, Wiltshire

Contents

List of Illustrations		vii
Index to Persons in Narrative		ix
Chronology		xi
	Introduction	1
1	From Merthyr to the Pyramids	5
2	Egypt and the Search for Coal	11
3	The Missing Years	27
4	Khartoum, Ivory and Slaves	37
5	Exploration and Trade	49
6	The Promise	63
7	The Journey	75
8	The Race	85
9	The Succour Dodge	101
10	A Very Public Quarrel	123
11	Unfinished Business	135
	Conclusion	141
	Notes	149
	Appendices	159
	Select Bibliography	171
	Index	175

List of Illustrations

Frontispiece   John Petherick, White Nile trader and explorer.   ii

1   Katherine, Petherick's wife and companion on the disastrous
    trek through the Central African wilderness to assist the Nile
    explorers Speke and Grant.   2

2   John Hanning Speke (1827–1864), first European to discover
    Lake Victoria, which he claimed was the fountain of the River
    Nile.   3

3   Sir Richard Francis Burton who after the first expedition to
    Central Africa repudiated Speke's claim that Lake Victoria was
    the source of the Nile.   3

4   A felucca, the workboat of the river Nile.   14

5   The Citadel in Cairo where Petherick received instructions
    from the Viceroy, Muhammad Ali Pasha, on where to search for
    coal in Egypt.   16

6   St Catherine's Monastery in the Sinai Desert, Petherick's base
    during his search for coal.   18

7   Petherick was hoisted up the wall in a wicker basket to the
    entrance to St Catherine's Monastery, thirty feet above the ground. 19

8   The Burning Bush at St Catherine's Monastery from where God,
    according to the Old Testament, spoke to Moses. Reputedly, the
    monastery is built on the site of the biblical burning bush.   20

9   Petherick's route through the Sinai desert.   22

10   Petherick's rough sketch map showing the separate routes taken
     by himself and Speke/Grant to Gondokoro in 1863.   35

11   The Sudd and the White Nile basin.   41

12   Cattle swim the Nile at the beginning of the Sudd swamp
     somewhere below Lake No, driven by natives in dugout canoes.   42

13   Nuer porters cross the Sudd carrying loads on their heads.   43

14   Nuer youths with spears and shields hunting hippopotamus in
     one of the Sudd's many papyrus-filled lagoons.   44

15   Dinka tribesmen at a funeral dance.   44

16   Native families in the Sudan on their way to a circumcision
     lodge.   58

17   The Azande (meaning 'great eaters') were believed to be
     cannibals, but Petherick found no evidence of this.   69

18   Sir Samuel Baker, hunter/explorer, who provided support for
     Speke and Grant when the Pethericks were reported murdered.   87

19   Lady Florence Baker (née Florenz Sass), the teenager who
     became Sir Samuel's mistress, then wife after he rescued her
     from a Transylvanian slave market.   87

Index to Persons in Narrative

Abil il-Majid: Petherick's most trusted agent, caught trafficking slaves.

Baker, Sir Samuel: wealthy big game hunter, explorer, and first European to sight Albert Nyanza.

Brownell, James: American doctor who joined the Petherick Expedition to Gondokoro.

Burton, Sir Richard Francis: linguist, explorer, diplomat, and leader of the first European expedition to the Central African lakes region.

De Malzac, Alphonse: French slave trader.

De Bono, Andrea: Maltese slave trader.

De Bono, Amabile (also Muso): Maltese slave trader.

Florence, Lady Baker: wife of Sir Samuel Baker and formerly a slave.

Kamrasi: King of the Unyoro (Western Uganda).

Kurshid Aga: slave trader accused by Petherick.

Muhammad Wad-el-Mek: mercenary commander at Falaro *zeriba* jointly owned by Petherick and Amabile de Bono.

Muhammad Ali Pasha: Viceroy of Egypt and the Sudan.

Murchison, Sir Rodney: President of the Royal Geographical Society and proponent of the Geological Timescale for calculating the age of the earth.

Mussaad: Petherick agent at Neambara *zariba* sent to find Speke and Grant.

Mutesa: King of Buganda (Uganda), where Speke spent four and a half months before discovering Ripon Falls only forty miles away.

Natterer, Josef: Austrian Vice-Consul in Khartoum.

Petherick, John: Welsh mining engineer, White Nile trader and explorer.

Petherick, Katherine: wife of John Petherick who accompanied him on his travels.

Rumanika: King of Karagwé (present day Tanzania) at whose palace Speke cavorted with fat native princesses.

Speke, John Hanning: wealthy big game hunter, explorer, and first European to sight Victoria Nyanza which he claimed was the source of the Nile.

Chronology

1813   13 June, John Petherick christened at St Tydfil's Parish Church, Merthyr.

1821   21 March, Richard Francis Burton born in Torquay, Devon.

8 June, Samuel White Baker born in London.

1827   4 May, John Hanning Speke born in Orleigh Court, Somerset.

1828   16 August, Katherine Petherick (née Edelmann) christened at St Matthews Church, Douglas, Isle of Man (not Malvern as she stated in census returns).

1845   Petherick leaves for Egypt.

1849   Petherick appointed British Vice-Consul in the Sudan.

1857–59   Burton/Speke Expedition to the lake regions.

1858   3 August, Speke reaches southern shore of Victoria Nyanza.

1859   Petherick returns to Britain after fourteen years in Egypt and the Sudan.

1860–63   Speke/Grant Expedition to Lake Victoria; leave for Zanzibar 27 April 1860.

1860   Petherick appointed British Consul in the Sudan.

31 October, Petherick marries widow Katherine Harriet Walshe (née Edelmann) at Brighton.

1861   February, Petherick publishes *Egypt, the Sudan and Central Africa*.

March, Samuel Baker arrives Egypt to 'commence an expedition to discover the source of the Nile with the hope of meeting the East African Expedition of Captains Speke and Grant'.

15 April, Bakers leave Cairo to explore Blue Nile.

2 May, Pethericks arrive in Alexandria, Egypt.

15 October, Pethericks arrive in Khartoum by Nile barge.

December, Petherick relief boats arrive in Gondokoro to await Speke/Grant.

1862   28 March, Pethericks leave Khartoum for Gondokoro.

11 June, Bakers arrive in Khartoum.

2 July, Pethericks abandon boats to proceed overland when only 150 miles from Gondokoro.

18 December, Bakers sail for Gondokoro; Pethericks reported dead.

1863   20 January, another three Petherick boats arrive at Gondokoro from Khartoum.

25 January, Pethericks reach station at Wayo; collect elephant tusks.

2 February, Bakers arrive at Gondokoro.

20 February, Pethericks reach Gondokoro eleven months after leaving Khartoum; dine with Speke, Grant and Baker.

26 February, Speke/Grant leave Gondokoro to return to England.

Speke publishes *Journal of the Discovery of the Source of the Nile*.

1864   Burton and James McQueen publish *The Nile Basin*.

15 September, Speke dies in a shooting accident.

16 September, Murchison announces Speke's death at Royal Geographical Society meeting, Bath.

1866   Baker publishes *The Albert N'yanza: Great Basin of the Nile and Explorations of the Nile Sources.*

1869   John and Katherine Petherick publish *Travels in Central Africa.*

1877   March, Katherine Petherick dies at St Austell, Cornwall, aged 49.

1882   15 July, John Petherick dies in lodging house in Kensington, aged 69.

Introduction

THE MAIN OUTLINES OF THE CLASSICAL AGE of heroic African exploration are well-known and can be clicked through like a set of lecture slides: from Captain John Hanning Speke's first glimpse of Lake Victoria, acclaimed as the 'source' of the Nile to Henry Morton Stanley's immortal words, 'Dr Livingstone, I presume?'

The problem with slides is that in focussing only on the most prominent and popular milestones the picture is incomplete and, on occasions, confused. In the case of Central Africa, this lack of definition, due to a shortage of source material from the 17th and 18th centuries, has meant that not everyone responsible for shedding light on the Dark Continent has received proper recognition.

John Petherick, the Welsh mining engineer from Merthyr Tydfil, was one such person. Whenever mentioned in the company of those elevated to the pantheon of celebrated African explorers – David Livingstone, Stanley, Captains Speke and James Grant, Sir Samuel Baker, Sir Richard Burton – his exploits seem mere footnotes in the margins of the main players. But if exploration is about going where no man has before, arguably Petherick covered more of Africa than even the missionary explorer Livingstone. But on the bicentenary of the birth of both men – 2013 – few, if any, will commemorate the man from Merthyr whose achievements remain mired in controversy, incrimination, and some elitism.

The Petherick portrayed in the literature of African exploration is that of the 'succour dodge': the man who dipped into the public purse to assist Speke and Grant discover the Holy Grail of African exploration – the source of the Nile – but then left them in the lurch. Worse still, the Welshman was accused of being a slave trader on the White Nile two decades after Britain banned it. However, in Egypt and the Sudan where Petherick spent almost seventeen years, slavery continued to flourish.

Not unnaturally, after such a length of time in remote and dangerous places, from the burning deserts of the Sinai to the disease-ridden swamps of Central Africa, Petherick's 'wild Arab look' was more suited to the ruffian world of Nile traders than polite Victorian society. The big man with the wicked pirate beard, close-set eyes squinting at some far horizon, spoke a different language to the gentleman explorer Speke with whom he had a monumental quarrel that destroyed his reputation. Whereas Speke's life was steeped in privilege, his aspirations lubricated by money and influence, Petherick's was touched by the heavy hand of an iron town teeming with the hard working and the destitute. His march through the African wilderness was driven not by any consideration for public acclaim but by a search for profit: from ivory or slaves, or both?

For ten years I've wrestled with telling the story of Petherick the Welsh adventurer, and his courageous wife Katherine: she a widow at 32 with two teenage daughters, he 47 when they married. Together, this remarkable couple stood shoulder to shoulder against dangers and privations beyond imagination in this day of tropical medicines, air ambulances, and four-wheel drive. The blank space at the centre of Victorian maps of the Dark Continent was shaped like a human heart – and for the Pethericks it bled!

But there is a truly bizarre coincidence behind this story. After being drawn to the saga of the Pethericks by a chance conversation with the archivist at Merthyr Public Library, I discovered my name was: John Petherick! My story starts not in Africa, not even Merthyr, or Cornwall where the Petherick family had its roots, but in

Figure 1. *(left) Katherine, Petherick's wife and companion on the disastrous trek through the Central African wilderness to assist the Nile explorers Speke and Grant.*

Figure 2. (*above*) *John Hanning Speke 1827–1864, first European to discover Lake Victoria, which he claimed was the fountain of the River Nile.*

Figure 3. (*right*) *Sir Richard Francis Burton, who after the first expedition to Central Africa repudiated Speke's claim that Lake Victoria was the source of the Nile.*

the Union Workhouse at Christchurch in Hampshire where in 1899 my grandmother gave birth to an illegitimate son entered in the workhouse register as Charles Petherick – my father. When his mother died not long afterwards from consumption, he was taken from the workhouse by a couple living in South Wales and assumed their name Humphries, a common enough practice before the legalisation of adoption. Is it surprising that I always wonder whether something is hidden behind the workhouse door about Petherick the Welsh adventurer!

But to start at the beginning, let the Petherick story – or as much as we know – tell itself.

John Humphries
Tredunnoc, Gwent
February 2013

CHAPTER 1

From Merthyr to the Pyramids

THE ELDEST OF SEVEN SURVIVING CHILDREN, John Petherick was born in 1813 in a 'smoke-tinted house' behind Merthyr Tydfil's Penydarren Ironworks where his father was a works agent. Following the well-beaten money trail from tin-mining in Cornwall to iron-making in Merthyr, his father and grandfather, both also John, migrated from Camborne to what was once the isolated valley home of a handful of poor Welsh farmers and ragged sheep but by the start of the 19th century was a boom town created by coal and ironstone. When Petherick was christened at St Tydfil's Parish Church on 13 June 1813, his father was one of an elite cadre of managers employed to run this industrial colossus on behalf of four powerful 'iron families'. As agent at Penydarren for William Forman and his absentee partner Alderman Thompson (Member of Parliament for Westminster), Petherick Senior dealt with the Crawshays at Cyfarthfa, the Guests at Dowlais and the Hills at Plymouth who from their mansions on the hill presided over a community where prosperity and poverty were only ever feet apart. In sharp contrast to the crabbed terraces clinging to the valley sides, the Petherick household had fine furniture, cut-crystal glasses, and paintings on the walls.

Nothing, however, could have shielded the younger Petherick from the turbulence of this frontier town. While never suffering the bleak circumstances of contemporaries, he did lose an infant brother and sister to the disease that assailed Merthyr, the fear and desperation that regularly stalked the town pressing upon the young man's adolescent consciousness, albeit in the company house on the other side of the tracks.[1] Just a few feet from his home, the road rose steeply towards the lava flows of Dowlais Top, the fire and brimstone of rapacious industry choking the valley. At the Cinder Hole, trams tipped red-hot waste from the coke ovens over man-made precipices ablaze with a thousand fires. Fanned by high winds, sheets of flame and clouds of acrid smoke spewed into the valley below, accompanied by the clanging hammers and the confused din of the massive machinery at the beating heart of the Black Domain.

Life could be short and brutal, but the inhabitants were fiercely independent with 'great strength ... dark minds ... strong passions and vigorous vices' – the *Merthyr Guardian* fretting over the 'little bastards' flooding the streets. Not surprisingly, Petherick emerged from the rough and tumble of early 19th century Merthyr with a reputation for having a heavy hand and strong conviction that physical explanation was sometimes necessary in an argument.

To control such people, the ironmasters had truck. The company shop – the only means of supplying isolated communities during the early days of the iron boom – was used to enslave workers in a monstrous cycle of debt and credit that left them beholden to their employers. 'If the masters had not had some hold over such a set of men and were to make them entirely independent by giving them complete control over their high wages, they would work just when and how they liked, and the capital embarked in the works would be at their mercy' was how one ironmaster justified this iniquity.[2]

Despite a huge influx of migrant workers from the surrounding countryside and from other parts of Britain, the predominant language of Merthyr in the first part of the 19th century was Welsh. Like his father, the younger Petherick almost certainly spoke it, even though an increasing number of people were persuaded to believe that Welsh was a barrier to progress and synonymous with illiteracy. His first encounter with the language was at Mr Shaw's school for infants at Turnpike Cottage, and afterwards at Taliesin Williams's school on the Glebeland where pupils devoted part of their studies to copying the Welsh language manuscripts of their headmaster's illustrious father, Edward Williams – best known by his Bardic name, Iolo Morganwg.[3] At Taliesin's, the young Petherick rubbed shoulders with the sons of the 19th century gang masters at the centre of the complex web of trades hired to run the ironworks and collieries. By then part of Merthyr's emerging middle-class, the 'butties' organized the teams of puddlers, shinglers, catchers, balers, moulders, and carriers, without whom production quickly ground to a standstill.

Precisely when he left Merthyr to study as a mining engineer at the Institute of Geology at Breslau University in eastern Prussia (now Poland) is uncertain but evidently the intention was to return and follow his father and grandfather into the iron industry, the only son who did so, if only briefly. All the surviving Petherick siblings would leave Merthyr for other parts of Wales and less demanding occupations as retailers and teachers. A younger brother, James, opted out entirely to live as a recluse. Hating the noise and graft of the ironworks, James is remembered as the 'Hermit of Mountain Ash' living in a mountain cottage at Cefn Pennar out of sight of the glowing blast furnaces. Dressed in rustic garb, and carrying a long staff, his fine white beard streaming in the wind, James was a familiar figure among the highways and byways studying the local flora and fauna. Reserved and respectful, he preferred enlightenment to confrontation, quite different from his impulsive elder brother whose impetuosity at Breslau University ended in a duel, and a rapier slash he carried to the grave.[4]

Petherick was probably fortunate to be at Breslau on 3 June 1831 and not at home where his father was thrust into the centre of the Merthyr Rising. As agent for Penydarren, Petherick Senior knew trouble was brewing. Not only did he employ some of the principal protagonists, he had spied upon them at a protest meeting at the Waun Fair a month previously. A white flag emblazoned with the slogan 'Reform the Parliament' was hoisted as speaker after speaker attacked the hated Court of Requests.[5] Life on credit had created an army of wage-slaves dreading the bailiff's knock – in one instance the mattress seized from beneath a dying woman.

Magistrates were locked in a council of war at the Castle Inn when, with the town ready to explode, a detachment of Argyll and Sutherland Highlanders arrived. The testimony of Petherick Senior as to what followed was generally considered the most detailed and accurate account of events, although strangely he was not called to testify at the subsequent trial. But his evidence at the inquest which preceded it helped convict Lewis Lewis (Lewsyn yr Heliwr, or Lewis the Huntsman) and Richard Lewis, immortalized as Dic Penderyn, the working class martyr hanged at Cardiff Prison for stabbing a soldier during the melee.

Petherick Senior was at the window of the Castle Inn alongside the 'Iron King' William Crawshay of Cyfarthfa and Josiah John Guest of Dowlais as the mob closed with the Highlanders defending the entrance. The previous day the Red Flag was raised for the first time in Britain by demonstrators ransacking houses to recover property confiscated by the Court of Requests. The Riot Act was read that evening after the Red Flag was shaken in the faces of the magistrates, and the home of a court official set alight. That same night, Petherick Senior was supervising production in the puddling forge at Penydarren when the mob burst in. 'Why stop the works?' he pleaded. 'To get better wages,' one replied. Another forced him to take the Red Fag, soaked in calf's blood, as a sign that he supported the uprising. 'I said if it would please him … I had no objection,' the man replying, 'That's right … you are now sworn in.'[6]

The Riot Act was read a second time the following morning when two thousand demonstrators besieged the Castle Inn. From a window on the first floor Petherick Senior had a grandstand view of the bloodbath that ensued:

> I saw some of the 93rd Regiment proceed in front of the inn along the pavement. They had bayonets fixed. The mob was considerably excited … pressing close upon the soldiers … Major Falls and another officer endeavouring to keep the mob from pressing on the men, begging them to stand off but they only gave way for a moment and came on again. I went into a passage of the inn and heard a soldier complain to an officer that he had been insulted by the mob. The officer said, 'Do your duty, and hold your tongue … if you do not be quiet and obey orders implicitly I will cut you down.' I then saw a man elevated on the shoulders of the mob who said they did not want it believed they would be satisfied with bread only … at which moment the mob cried, 'Caws gyda bara,' that is 'Cheese with bread.' Then the same man said, 'As well as bread we must have money to buy cheese and shoes and clothes, money to pay rent and for beer …'[7]

Petherick identified Lewis Lewis clinging to an iron lamp post and shouting in Welsh, 'Listen boys! They say they have brought the soldiers here for their protection; if every one of you is of my mind we will show they are not a sufficient protection.' Some carried heavy iron bludgeons while others waved the Red Flag like battlefield colours in the faces of the soldiers before rushing forward propelled violently from behind. The mob drew back and rushed a second time, according to Petherick:

> About three or four attacked each soldier … The officer distributed his men among the front rooms, telling them clearly, 'Recollect men, your orders are not to fire unless commanded by an officer.' Three or four of the soldiers were lying on the ground (in the street) … the mob (was) certainly getting the better of them. The officer looked a second time through the window and gave the order to 'Fire' … when the smoke cleared the mob had begun to retreat and I saw four or five bodies lying in the street opposite the front of the inn, bleeding.[8]

Petherick counted the bodies of eight or nine rioters in the street strewn with bludgeons and rocks. The mob attacked a final time, firing at the hotel from behind a bank a hundred yards away, the musket balls whistling around Petherick as he dived for cover. After three-quarters of an hour the shooting stopped, and the dead rioters were taken to the hotel stables.

The battle was by no means over. Fearing a general insurrection across the Black Domain, magistrates and soldiers retreated to Penydarren House, home of the Forman family: a fortified redoubt from which the Highlanders would attempt to reclaim Merthyr. For the next eight days the rioters held the town until the Highlanders, reinforced by the Royal Glamorgan Militia and Yeomanry confronted the insurgents at Cefn. Not a shot was fired. The crowd backed off and the insurgency collapsed.

Petherick Senior sympathized with the plight of the rioters, commenting, 'I am not in distress myself but I know those who are so.' Recriminations were widespread after Richard Lewis (Dic Penderyn) was hanged pleading his innocence with his last breath, and Lewis Lewis transported to Van Dieman's Land for life.

Perhaps they were ostracized but the Pethericks left Merthyr two years later announcing the auction of their property in the *Merthyr Guardian* on 26 October 1833. The family sold almost everything, ranging from 'a very elegant dinner service ... and superior assortment of paintings, prints and books ... and an extensive collection of mineralogical specimens.' Some of the paintings were the work of Petherick Senior, an accomplished self-taught artist drawing his subjects from the 19th century industrial landscape of the valleys.[9]

Whatever the reason, Petherick Senior quit a well-paid job at Penydarran to become manager of the newly-opened Pyle Ironworks. Within a year the works was in financial difficulties and he returned to Merthyr, not to Penydarren, but as manager of the neighbouring Rhymney Ironworks, another venture in which 'Billy Ready Money,' the name the City coined for Petherick's entrepreneurial former employer, William Forman, had invested. After seven years at Rhymney, he moved finally to the Cambrian Ironworks at Maesteg, later renamed the Llynfi Works. The project was a financial disaster and by the 1851 census Petherick Senior was unemployed and living at 62 Eastgate Street, Bridgend with wife Martha, their last surviving daughter Mary (30), youngest son William (25), and a live-in servant.

After completing his studies at the University of Breslau, the younger Petherick obtained a position as mining engineer for a complex of coalmines owned by the English and German Mining Company in Germany's Hartz Mountains. By chance, he was living at Dillenburg when Sir Roderick Murchison and his collaborator Professor Adam Sedgwick arrived to study the local geology. Before championing African exploration as president of

the Royal Geographical Society, Murchison was a prominent geologist who
with Sedgwick shaped the heroic age of modern geology by proposing the
fossil record as a means of grouping geological formations, as opposed to
the traditionalists who subscribed to a grand cosmological explanation
for the formation of the earth's crust. For this reason they visited Wales
frequently, Sedgwick spending one summer in the Cambrian Mountains
rock hunting with Charles Darwin before Darwin sailed aboard the *Beagle*
on his historic voyage.[10]

Sedgwick's rock-hunting in Wales led him in 1835 to identify the
Cambrian period in the geological timescale, followed closely by Murchison's
classification of the overlapping Silurian period. Their next objective was
to prove the existence of another geological period – the Devonian – and
to demonstrate its universality they had travelled to the Hartz Mountains
in Germany's Rhineland in 1839 where with the assistance of an 'English
miner' they found evidence to support their theory.

Petherick Junior was the 'English miner' mentioned by Murchison in a
letter to his wife describing his 'famous excursion on foot, headed by a little
broad-shouldered clever Prussian *bergmeister* who, booted and spurred, led
the way (pipe in mouth, hammer in hand), followed by S [Sedgwick], De
Verneuil [a French geologist], myself and an English miner.' That evening at
an inn in Dillenburg, they enjoyed a session around the piano after dining
with the 'young English miner and his sisters', most probably the innkeep-
er's daughters.[11]

For health reasons, Petherick later quit his job in Germany, travelling first to Switzerland and then France, afterwards returning to Wales,
first to work for a short time in the iron industry, before taking the spa
waters at Llandrindod Wells. While recovering, he was recommended by
a Cardiff engineer named Gallaway as a suitable candidate to fill a commission from Muhammad Ali Pasha, Viceroy of Egypt and the Sudan
to search for coal in the desert. The Viceroy was also constructing a
railway from Cairo to Suez and Gallaway his recruiting agent in Wales.
The young Welsh mining engineer seized the opportunity to escape the
Black Domain.

CHAPTER 2

Egypt and the Search for Coal

TEA PLANTERS RETURNING TO CEYLON from home leave and employees of the East India Company comprised most of the passengers aboard the *S.S. Great Liverpool* departing Southampton for Egypt in 1845. For Petherick, the acute sense of adventure was mixed with foreboding, not knowing for how long he was severing links with Britain, family and friends. Communications with the far reaches of Empire were still protracted, news from Africa taking eight weeks to reach the *Times* by overseas mail. By the time Petherick returned, the Crimea War was over after great loss of life; nations shaken by political upheaval and revolution; the traditional doctrine that man was the product of divine intervention challenged by Charles Darwin; and America on the verge of civil war over the emancipation of millions of slaves.

Britain had banned the infamous Triangular Trade between itself, West Africa and the Americas in 1806. Moral outrage over the transportation of Black Africans shackled and yoked together like animals, stacked like sacks of flour in wooden hulks had produced one of the undisputed achievements of an era that once subscribed to the notion that slavery was ordained by God. The belief that some had the right to 'possess, buy, sell, discipline, transport, liberate, dispose of others' was finally extirpated by the 1833 Act making slave ownership, as well as trafficking, a capital offence throughout the British Empire. No longer was it possible for Black Africans bought in West Africa with cheap manufactured goods from Birmingham to be exchanged in the New World for tobacco, sugar, and cotton: a trade that netted a staggering £13 billion (at 2005 prices) for the British and American commercial, political and aristocratic classes that dominated it for two centuries. No longer were British subjects permitted to own slaves. Not surprisingly, its abolition left the country feeling a deep sense of national atonement and with a new moral compass directing evangelical enthusiasm towards other important social issues of the 19th century.

Despite having spent a large part of his adult life in Germany, Petherick would have known that in Britain the abolitionists held sway: that the British Anti-Slavery Society had helped rid the west, theoretically at least, of a foul and detestable crime against humanity. But this great wave of emancipation had not yet washed ashore in North Africa when the *S. S. Great Liverpool* threaded its way into the harbour at Alexandria through scores of small boats ferrying merchandise ashore. Slaves were everywhere, employed as domestic servants at almost every level of Egyptian society: by Muslims, Christians and Jews alike, a status symbol 'as essential to respectability amongst one's neighbours as [was] a servant for menial work in European families.'[1] Even the French ambassador owned slaves, while one consular agent made a fortune from trading them.[2] The most valuable were eunuchs – boys aged between eight and ten castrated in the Sudan for sale to the harems of the Middle East.

The Egyptian government more or less ignored what was happening in the west. The Viceroy while declaring himself opposed to slavery was not inclined to interfere with an institution sanctioned by the Qur'an. When the public slave market in Khartoum was closed as a gesture to western sensibilities, the trade transferred to Kaka, a remote Shillook village on the White Nile. Even though the slave traffic between the Sudan and Egypt was prohibited in 1854, the ban was not enforced because of powerful slave-owning interests. While the British Anti-Slavery Society did press the Government to act, the Foreign Office was reluctant to interfere with Islamic chattel slavery about which the abolitionists knew little, and British diplomats not a great deal more. The slave trade was institutionalized, freely and openly pursued when Petherick arrived in 1845, and the Nile a slave highway supplying markets in Egypt, Turkey and across the Eastern Desert and Red Sea to Arabia. A quarter of the poor wretches perished before reaching their destination, those too sick to travel tossed into the Nile, and the diseased slaughtered to avoid infection spreading to the rest of the 'cargo'.[3] The principal source of slaves was the tribal area southwest of Khartoum, in particular the Nuba Mountains of Kordofan from which thousands were taken in *razzias* (slave hunts) each year.[4] Petherick would spend five years in Kordofan's capital El Obeid buying and selling gum arabic – a valuable extract from acacia trees used in manufacturing – but never slaves, he insisted.

So embedded, however, was slavery in Arab and Black African society that the missionary explorer and anti-slavery campaigner David Livingstone, despairing at the sight of a slave woman executed because she was unable to take another step, was convinced that the only way to liberate Africa was through European colonisation, his famous three 'C's': Commerce, Christianity, and Civilisation. As it happened, the strategic and economic objectives of the European powers were more important than action against the slave trade in Egypt and the Sudan. For Britain, the scramble for Africa was about planting the flag and the exploitation of resources without attention to local cultural and ethnic groups. By the mid-nineteenth century the East African slave trade was worth more than the combined trade in palm oil, gum arabic and ivory. Slaves were a currency for paying taxes as well as the backbone of the Viceroy's Black African regiments. It was hardly surprising that when Petherick landed in Alexandria slaves were everywhere, hauling and heaving goods on the dockside, and escorting their owners through the bustling alleyways and *souks*.

Whatever romantic notions Petherick had of Egypt's mystic pyramids rising out of a yellow plain dotted with clumps of tall palm trees, of the Spinx brooding over a tranquil Nile, were drowned by the yelling chorus of donkey boys shrieking, 'Ride, sir! Donkey, sir! I say, sir!' in excellent English at the passengers disembarking from the *S. S. Great Liverpool*. With a street urchin screaming at his side, and his boots dragging through the dust, Petherick was delivered to his destination at a brisk seven miles an hour. Undignified, but the fastest way to navigate Alexandria's crowded alleyways.

The city in the mid-nineteenth century did not strike Petherick as particularly Eastern, having the ambience of a continental capital thronged by Jews, Armenians and Europeans. The more prosperous parts were characteristically French, a legacy of the Napoleonic occupation, but otherwise there was little to detain visitors from hurrying on to the pyramids at Giza. What little that remained after several earthquakes devastated one of the seven wonders of the ancient world, the Lighthouse of Alexandria (the Pharos), was removed in the 15th century for recycling while the city's other main attraction, the Great Library, was burned down by Julius Caesar.

The journey from Alexandria to Cairo was by barge along the Mahmoudieh Canal to join the Rosetta branch of the River Nile. At Enfe, passengers transferred to fast steamers for the 120-mile journey upriver, sailing between muddy banks across a vast delta tinged with the green shoots of spring. At the river's margins children splashed, Arabs bathed donkeys in the shallows, while their women beat the life out of washing on flat stones at the edges of the cool, shining surface. In the distance, the pyramids of Giza dazzled in the bright sunshine, matching every traveller's expectation.

Figure 4. *A felucca, the workboat of the river Nile.*

The Nile was alive with feluccas. The long, low workboats of the river ferried cotton and other merchandise to Boulak where tall factory chimneys testified to the Viceroy's modernisation of ancient Egypt and where donkeys waited to transport the weary travellers into the city over the Ezbekieh plain dotted with the villas of rich pashas lolling on cushions as they drove past in *barouches*. From Cairo, most passengers from the *S. S. Great Liverpool* took the Overland Route across the desert by horse-drawn sand sledges, stopping occasionally at rest stations for iced champagne, canapés, and European mineral water before joining steamers waiting at Port Suez on the Red Sea. Until the opening of the Suez Canal, the Overland Route reduced the journey time to India from three months to forty days by avoiding the voyage around the Cape of Good Hope.

After bidding his fellow passengers bon voyage, Petherick checked into Cairo's Hôtel d'Orient, French-owned, managed by an Italian and patronized by the English. His contract with the Viceroy was for three years but he anticipated returning to Wales sooner, if, as he suspected, there was as much chance of finding coal at the top of the Pyramids as in the Egyptian deserts. Instead, he stayed for fourteen years, mostly in southern Sudan, a hostile, disease-infested empty space rarely visited by Europeans; those who did fortunate to escape with their lives. If nothing else, Petherick's sojourn would be an exceptional feat of human endurance.

Almost always fully booked by transit passengers between London and Bombay, Hôtel d'Orient provided a quasi-French menu of ragouts and fricandeaux while remaining a slice of old England. Moustachioed majors in dress uniform, and civilians sporting cravats, waistcoats and white kid-gloves accompanied by pale-faced ladies with ringlets sipping glasses of pale ale gathered for dinner each evening. Afterwards, the ladies retired leaving the gentlemen to smoke Bengal cheroots and drink pale French brandy mixed with hot water and sugar. Mosquitoes were the only 'natives' to intrude upon this quintessential scene, their bloody visitations evident in the light of day.

The following morning Petherick was escorted from the hotel for his first audience with Muhammad Ali Pasha, the Albanian mercenary who rose through the ranks of the Ottoman Empire to become Viceroy of Egypt. As a young officer Muhammad Ali Pasha was sent to Egypt by the Ottomans in 1801 to repulse Napoleon's invasion. In the anarchy that followed the withdrawal of the French he declared himself pasha, leaving a reluctant Sultan no alternative but recognize him as Viceroy. To this Muhammad Ali Pasha would add a large part of the Sudan, establishing Khartoum at the confluence of the Blue and White Niles as the military and administrative capital of the territory.

On assuming the position of Viceroy he immediately purged the Mamluks, a powerful military caste loyal to the Ottoman Sultans. Invited to a feast at the Viceroy's Citadel in the Muqattam Hills, the Mamluk princes were trapped in a narrow alleyway and slaughtered. The survivors fled south to establish a slave state until the Viceroy completed their annihilation, in the process seizing Kordofan for Egypt. By the time Petherick settled in

Figure 5. *The Citadel in Cairo where Petherick received instructions from the Viceroy, Muhammad Ali Pasha, on where to search for coal in Egypt.*

Kordofan to trade gum arabic, its capital, El Obeid, had one of the largest slave markets in the whole of Africa.

The dynasty founded by Muhammad Ali Pasha lasted until the revolution of 1952. The 'father' of modern Egypt, the Viceroy built roads, railways and canals, and transformed Egyptian cotton production. But what was needed most in 1845 was coal to replace that imported from what was then the largest known coalfield in the world. It was no great surprise he turned to South Wales for help.

Petherick's audience was at Shubra, a miniature Versailles on the banks of the Nile. After half an hour's carriage drive from Cairo, he was led into a pavilion of glistening white marble alongside a large pool. Seated on a raised divan beneath a ceiling decorated with paintings of the Viceroy and his sons, Muhammad Ali gestured to the Welshman to sit directly opposite his dark, searching gaze. Bowing deferentially, Petherick waited.

The Viceroy explained through an interpreter:

I have sent for you to travel in my country to search for minerals, but particularly for coal, of which I stand much in need. You have been very highly recommended to me, and I hope you will be successful in your researches. I have a manufactory at Boulak, which I wish you to see; and I want to enlarge it when you have found coal for me, that I may make guns and steam engines, and feel myself independent of England. I have several of your countrymen in my employ. As soon as you have reposed from the fatigues of your voyage, I wish you to travel over my country for which I will give you every facility.

The Viceroy paused, and smiled before adding with a chuckle that Petherick had a rival: a French mining engineer had also been employed to search for coal. He continued:

Although I have great confidence in Englishmen, there are no such inveterate enemies as the English and the French ... and I want to get up a little fight in Egypt between you and the Frenchman, from which I hope to reap the advantage. Depend upon it, the victor who first discovers coal shall be handsomely rewarded.

With that Petherick was dismissed. Until sent for, he was to amuse himself in Cairo.[5]

The call to attend the Viceroy at his official residence and symbol of power, the Citadel, came a few days later. Petherick waited in line with a gaggle of functionaries wearing large diamond stars denoting their place in the ruling hierarchy. When his time came, the Welshman was shown into Muhammad Ali Pasha's offices, the Viceroy sitting cross-legged on a low divan, the very large Mamluk at his side swatting flies. Beckoning Petherick to take a seat, the Viceroy explained how a shaft had been sunk in a petrified forest not far from Cairo. Petherick was told to inspect it the next day.

'Afterwards you will come to me at Shubra and give me your opinion on the probability of finding coal there. I am told that judging from the petrifaction of the wood on the surface it is sure to exist in a carbonised state underneath,' said the Viceroy confidently. A discussion followed about where coal was found in Britain and at what depth, how many men were employed to mine it, and how long reserves were expected to last.[6]

The next day Petherick descended to the bottom of an 800-foot shaft sunk through thick beds of blue marl wholly incompatible with the existence of coal-bearing seams.[7] That evening at Shubra Palace the Viceroy was playing cards with three grey-bearded, diamond-encrusted Turks in a *kiosk* in the gardens. Laying down his cards as Petherick entered, he asked excitedly whether the pit had been examined. 'Yes, but I do not consider there is the remotest chance of discovering coal,' Petherick blurted. With fire blazing in his Albanian eyes, the Viceroy struck the table angrily, sending the

Figure 6. *St Catherine's Monastery in the Sinai Desert, Petherick's base during his search for coal.*

cards flying. 'Then I'll sink a thousand yards!' he declared, at which point Petherick bid his salaams and left quickly.[8]

The weeks passed. The only word from the Citadel was that Petherick had been promoted to honorary lieutenant-colonel in Muhammad Ali's army. Not long afterwards he adopted the costume of a high-ranking Turk, a waist-length sleeved jacket with sash and riding britches. Add to this his wild, luxuriant nut-brown beard and it was no surprise he was often mistaken for a Turk. 'Dressed in Turkish costume,' he later recalled, 'I was always taken for a Turk. On many occasions when I explained that my country was an island in the salt sea, the women were lost in wonder and surprise, and could not imagine what on earth had induced me to travel so far from home.'

On being summoned to the Citadel, the Viceroy asked what part of Egypt Petherick intended to explore for coal. Without hesitation the Welshman replied, 'Arabia Petraea' – the arid deserts of the Sinai Peninsula and the Negev, extending from the shores of the Red Sea northwards into Palestine. That Petherick chose to follow the route taken by Moses when leading the Israelites out of Egypt had no significance. The claims by the Swiss explorer John Lewis Burckhardt to having discovered large outcrops of petrified wood and the remains of ancient blast furnaces for smelting iron and copper during his travels in the Sinai thirty years previously were more important to Petherick than the Old Testament account of Moses receiving the Ten Commandments on Mount Sinai.

The Sinai was a region of constant tribal warfare at the very limit of the Viceroy's realm. To secure safe passage for the Petherick Expedition, Muhammad Ali Pasha addressed firmans (decrees) to his governors at Suez and Aqaba, and to various tribal chiefs as far as the borders of Syria in the north and the Hedja (Saudi Arabia) in the east. Each was made responsible for escorting the Petherick Expedition safely through his territory. In addition, the patriarch of the Greek Orthodox Church in Alexandria gave the Welshman a letter of introduction to the monks at St Catherine's Monastery. With twenty-five camels, provisions, tents and engineering equipment, and accompanied by Arab engineers and two slaves, Petherick left Cairo for Port Suez on the shores of the Red Sea.[9] His rival, the French engineer

Figure 7. *Petherick was hoisted up the wall in a wicker basket to the entrance to St Catherine's Monastery thirty feet above the ground.*

Figure 8. *The Burning Bush at St Catherine's Monastery from where God, according to the Old Testament, spoke to Moses. Reputedly, the monastery is built on the site of the biblical burning bush.*

M. Noetinger headed in the opposite direction: into Upper Egypt where there was a long-established tradition of mining. Petherick would follow the same parched *wadis* (river valleys) to St Catherine's as Burckhardt, and using the monastery as a base strike eastwards into the barren wilderness of Wadi Araba, the great desert valley running from the Gulf of Aqaba to the Dead Sea and Petra, the 6th century B.C. Nabataen city buried by the sand until rediscovered by Burckhardt in 1812.[10]

The Sinai Peninsula is one of the most geologically complex regions on the planet, bounded on two sides by drowned branches of Africa's Rift Valley – the Red Sea – and elsewhere a labyrinth of narrow, arid rock-bound valleys surrounded by gaunt peaks and dreary ridges; a scene of utmost desolation deserving of its Biblical description as the 'great and terrible wilderness'. After sudden thunderstorms, flash floods briefly feed oases of palms and tamarisk trees. Otherwise, it is has the appearance of one gigantic quarry.

After stopping briefly at Station Number 4 on the Overland Route for supper, Petherick raced through the night to arrive before dawn at the Transit Hotel. Suez was no place to linger, P&O's Transit Hotel a refuge from the appalling climate and squalor. More Arabian than Egyptian, most of the town was abandoned, its walls in ruins. The air was foul, the barren wasteland on both sides filled with stagnant, stinking pools left by the tide. As a defence against fever, the inhabitants, mostly traders from Arabia and Syria drank copious quantities of brandy, which seemed only to hasten their demise. Water from the nearest wells turned putrid in a matter of days.

The Governor at Suez was instructed by Muhammad Ali Pasha to provide Petherick with a steamship to transport supplies and equipment across the twelve miles of the Gulf to Tor, a journey usually lasting a couple of hours. The ship was waiting but the Arab captain and engineer refused to sail. It was unsafe, they said, and to serve aboard such a boat was dishonourable. After listening quietly while puffing on his pipe, the governor turned to the captain, and said, 'I have no doubt your representations will meet with the immediate attention of his Excellency, the Minister of the Interior.' From his tone, the crew knew exactly what to expect. Unless the ship sailed immediately, they would suffer the *bastinado* – hung from a beam, and the soles of their feet beaten to the bone.

Next morning, a smoking chimney meant the engine was fixed but not Petherick's cabin, which was uninhabitable, filthy beyond description. Instead of two hours it took two days to cross the Gulf of Suez to Tor, with frequent stops for running repairs, every vibration shaking a screw loose. Tor, once an important port on the route to India, was deserted, a boat delivering provisions for the monks at St Catherine's Monastery the only regular visitor. Otherwise it was home to a handful of Arab fishermen and their families squatting in an abandoned date plantation.

From the barren coastal plain behind Tor, a mountain range runs northwest: a vast area of raw peaks, fossilized river valleys, and dried up gorges streaked azure, pink, yellow, and deep blue disappearing into the rust-coloured horizon. In this wilderness formed by ancient eruptions and earthquakes, Petherick was expected to find coal to fuel the engines of the Egyptian industrial revolution. The Welshman had learned his geology amongst the carboniferous limestone of South Wales with its coal seams formed from peat bogs. The granite escarpments of the Sinai were created when the world was a supercontinent – Gondwana – and covered only in a microbial crud.

Tor was a searing wall of heat. With nowhere to hide along the shore, Petherick pitched camp beneath a clump of date palms, waiting in the shade while his rugs, provisions and cooking utensils were carried from the beach by villagers. Most were half-blinded by ophthalmia, an infectious disease rife among people without sufficient water to wash. Believing Petherick to be a doctor, they pleaded for help, which he gave by bathing their sores in vinegar disguised with a little eau-de-cologne. 'If it did no good, it could do no harm,' he recalled.

The Bedouin bodyguard arrived later that day: a local sheikh and a couple of dozen men mounted on dromedaries. At his hip, each man carried a long, broad-bladed curved knife, and across his shoulders a matchlock rifle. The woollen shawl each Bedouin wore as a turban became a blanket wherever he lay down in the desert to sleep. All were strong and in the prime of life apart from the sheikh, whose long white beard betrayed, notwithstanding a muscular frame, that he was drifting into old age.

The next morning before the sun rose, Petherick mounted a dromedary for the first time, the see-sawing movement not unpleasant once accustomed to the 'ship of the desert'. But no sooner had they struck out across the barren plain beyond Tor and the air turned heavy and oppressive, the temperature soaring to 54°C (129°F), humidity dropping like a stone to less than 10 per cent. Great clouds of sand were blown into their faces forcing them to dismount and find cover. The *simoom*, the 'poison wind', was a suffocating blast that heated the body faster than it could dispose of it through perspiration. Sunstroke was common. The Bedouins squatting in the cover of a solitary cedar tree pulled their shawls over their heads and waited for the storm to pass leaving the camels to find shelter behind a patch

Figure 9. *Petherick's route through the Sinai desert.*

of scrubby acacia bushes. Petherick did the same, eventually emerging from the sand as though from the grave, eyes inflamed, face bloated, lips parched.

Petherick arrived at St Catherine's without further incident on 11 June 1845. Declining the monks' offer of accommodation he pitched camp in a small garden on a raised terrace adjacent to the monastery at the foot of the bold granite peaks of Mount Sinai. A fortified castle surrounded by high walls and defensive towers – sacred to Christians, Jews and Moslems alike – the monastery had twenty monks and just one entrance: a trap door in the wall thirty feet above the ground through which Petherick entered after being hauled up in a wicker basket. The Welshman appears to have had little interest in St Catherine's, the site of the Burning Bush from which God spoke to Moses. He was also totally unaware that the German scholar and archaeologist Constantin von Tischendorf had on a visit a few months earlier made one of great Biblical discoveries of the 19th century in the monastery library. From a wastepaper basket, Tischendorf recovered several leaves of parchment later identified as part of the earliest Greek translation of the Bible, dating from the 4th century, and equal in importance to the Codex Vaticanus, the most widely used version of the early Greek Bible. For Biblical scholars searching for the earliest apostolic text on which the Christian faith was founded, the St Catherine's discovery was a crucial piece in the jigsaw of documentary evidence proving the existence of Christ. On subsequent visits Tischendorf acquired most of the 964 surviving pages of the Codex Sinaiticus: half the Greek Old Testament (the Septuagint), the complete New Testament, together with the Epistle of Barnabas, and parts of the Shepherd of Hermas.[11]

Leaving the monastery, Petherick headed eastwards towards the Gulf of Aqaba to explore the dried-up river beds for signs of coal. The nearer to the coast the more nervous his bodyguard became until the Bedouins refused to travel any further into the territory of a tribe with whom there was a blood feud. Fearing desertion, he took hold of their leader and beat him with a stick until the Bedouins agreed to continue but only as far as Aqaba where they immediately decamped to be replaced by others to accompany Petherick on the final leg of the expedition up Wadi Araba as far as the lost city of Petra in present day Jordan. The night before they left, and following several glasses of *araki*, sleep proved impossible. The Arabs assigned to guard Petherick were drunk and noisy, ignoring his protestations and in desperation he bounded from the tent wearing only slippers and gave chase, planting a right-hander on the temple of the first man he caught. After this, there was no further disturbance – only the murmur of the sea across the beach.

The Petherick Expedition entered Wadi Araba armed to the teeth, the Bedouins scanning the horizon for signs of trouble. A wilderness of shifting sand dunes and gravel plains, the valley stretched for more than a hundred miles from the Gulf of Aqaba to the Dead Sea, enclosed on either side by parallel chains of bleached red sandstone peaks like the bleeding knuckles of an upraised fist. When it rained two rivers flowed but only briefly, one emptying into the Red Sea, the other lost in the sands.

The first sign of trouble was a group of Arabs calling for assistance from a rocky outcrop up ahead. While the Bedouins rode out to investigate, Petherick waited. Hearing shots, he jabbed his stirrup irons into his horse's flanks. As he got nearer, some half-naked Arabs wearing only cloths around their waists sprang out of the sand but were driven off by his Bedouins. Such was the lawlessness of Wadi Araba that geological exploration was impossible, every rock suspected of concealing a bandit. But before retreating Petherick examined an ancient copper smelter which judging from the amount of slag waste was once a substantial operation. But where the ore came from, and the fuel to smelt it, no one could say. After four months criss-crossing the Sinai, all the Welshman had to show the Viceroy was a small amount of carboniferous matter mixed with marl – not enough to boil a cup of tea!

On its return to Cairo, the expedition crossed from Sinai into Egypt near Gezeeret el Yahood (Island of the Jews), reputedly the spot where Moses parted the Red Sea to allow the Israelites to escape. It was here that Petherick first encountered the 'manna' from heaven credited with saving the Israelites from starvation. The shiny white drops of a gum-like substance exuded by acacia trees are more commonly-known as gum arabic, used at that time in Egypt for breadmaking. The Sinai gum was no bigger than garden peas with a sweetish taste, and harvested only every fifth year. The acacia growing in Kordofan to which Petherick would later attribute his financial success as a Nile trader was far more productive.

In Cairo Petherick waited apprehensively for the Viceroy's call. On being summoned to the Citadel and motioned to a seat after the customary salutations, the Welshman told the Viceroy that in his opinion there was no chance of finding coal in the Sinai.

'Ah, the Frenchman has been more fortunate,' replied the Viceroy showing Petherick some pieces of coal. 'What do you think of them? He is now on his way to France to procure boring implements.'

Putting a hand in his pocket Petherick pulled out his own small parcel of samples, as good as the Frenchman's, he told the Viceroy, but worthless because coal did not exist in sufficiently large quantities. The Viceroy, who by then was displaying symptoms of the dementia from which he died two years later, was finally persuaded to abandon the mine sunk outside Cairo.

From October 1845 until the following February Petherick awaited new instructions. Bored and impatient, he joined some European friends for a spot of tomb robbing at Saqqara, the vast burial ground outside the ancient Egyptian capital at Memphis. Descending thirty feet by rope into a burial chamber, and after picking their way across mounds of bones, they hauled the undamaged carcasses of two embalmed bulls to the surface, selling one to a private museum in Britain. 'The great destruction of the mummies,' wrote Petherick later, 'was sufficient proof that the place although but recently opened must have been ransacked at some earlier period, possibly by the Romans in search of gold, which some mummy pits were supposed to contain.'[12]

Petherick's next excursion was down the Nile to hunt wild boar in the delta. A strong northerly wind had forced the crew of the felucca to make fast alongside a village where a ferry packed with women and donkeys was setting off to cross the river. The boat had scarcely left the shore when it capsized but instead of helping the women struggling in the water Petherick's crew were more concerned about the donkeys. Angrily, he snatched up a *nabout* – a wooden club – and set about the crew, one of whom ignoring the clouts across his head and shoulders continued his struggle to save a donkey. Only a furious beating persuaded the Arab to release the animal by which time it was too late to save a mother and child from being swept away.[13]

The Viceroy refused to give up the search for coal. His next assignment for Petherick was Egypt's Eastern Desert, a wilderness drier and more sterile than the Sinai. The desert extended eastwards from the bank of the Nile to an ancient range of mountains running parallel to the Red Sea. There was even less chance of finding coal here since the geology was shaped long before the carboniferous period. Nevertheless, on 15 June 1846 Petherick led an expedition from Thebes (Luxor) into a wilderness where mountains were worn to the knuckle, streaked red and bluish-green, and the barren plains littered with ghostly piles glistening like snow in the moonlight.

The Welshman was accompanied by Sheikh Ali, a 'fine, handsome twenty-five year old with dark complexion and coal-black sparkling eyes', dressed in long calico shirts reaching to his ankles, his hands buried inside immensely wide sleeves. At his waist Sheikh Ali carried a straight sword like a claymore which he suspended by a strap from the shoulder when walking. A pair of pistols hung in holsters at his waist. Besides the young Sheikh, Petherick had a personal servant, a pipe-bearer, and an interpreter responsible to the Viceroy for auditing the accounts. The best of the guides was Karag who blindfolded was able to identify other members of the expedition by reading their footprints in the sand.

Several weeks into the journey some of the Bedouins were taken ill after drinking tainted water. Petherick, who only ever drank water carried from the Nile in personal containers, was fine and while Karag was sent to look for a well, he pressed ahead with Sheikh Ali and a second, less experienced guide. Soon they were hopelessly lost in the wilderness of bleak and rugged hills, not a living creature or plant of any kind in sight. After scrambling down another rubble-strewn gorge, and squeezing their dromedaries through a narrow passage between high cliff walls, they saw shimmering in the distance what resembled a white tent which the guide was sent to investigate, while Petherick and the Sheikh sheltered beneath the burned branches of a leafless tree. The tent was a large white boulder – and a mouthful of water was all they had left.

The next day they were luckier. After rounding a rocky outcrop they came across a camel browsing on some scrub, and not far away a Bedouin tent. Saddles and empty water skins hung from the branches of a tree – and in the sand the footprints of a man and woman but no sign of either. Suddenly, a pack of yelping dogs flew at them, followed by a flock of sheep driven by an old woman. A few minutes later the husband appeared, tall and elderly, face hewn from the rugged mountains. Without being asked, the man mounted Petherick's dromedary and set off to fill their skins at a remote well. In the meantime, his wife offered them a pot of sour milk, all she had, their goats dry from feeding on the sparse vegetation. The couple had no children, and spent their lives herding goats, sheep and camels in the mountains, rarely ever venturing into the valley below. Any surplus milk was turned into butter by shaking it to and fro in a skin and purifying it over a slow fire. In the spring, the husband drove his fat sheep and young camels to the towns along the Nile to exchange for grain. Money was of no use to the Bedouins. When offered coffee by Petherick, they refused. Never having tasted coffee, they thought it too late to start.

The next day the old man led them to a well where the remainder of the expedition was waiting. Angry with the guide for losing the trail, the Bedouins took away his whip – his badge of office – and ceremonially buried it in the sand.[14]

CHAPTER 3

The Missing Years

PETHERICK'S FINAL ASSIGNMENT from the aging Viceroy was to prepare an expedition for Persia. A few days later Muhammad Ali Pasha changed his mind – no great surprise to the Welshman accustomed to the Viceroy's sudden impulses. Instead, he was to investigate ancient iron workings in Kordofan, close to the Sudanese border with Darfur. The Kordofanese traditionally made iron goods to trade for produce from the Nile Valley. But on Petherick's first visit in 1847 the provincial capital El Obeid was better known as a slave market located on two of the most important slave routes in Africa: northwards to the Mediterranean, the other down the Nile to Egypt and Arabia.

After disembarking camels and supplies on the west bank of the river, Petherick set off across an arid plain dotted with thickets of acacia bushes burnt brown by the sun. El Obeid was a ten-day trek beneath cloudless skies, the suffocating heat bleaching the skeletons of animals and men scattered along the route and tormenting the living with mirages of clear, cool water dancing at the edge of consciousness. About half the size of Texas, Kordofan has no permanent rivers, only large stagnant pools teeming with leeches at the end of the wet season (July to September) which arrives like a blast from a hot furnace – a suffocating wind snatching at the throat followed by the crash of thunder and lightning before torrential downpours flood the thirsty desert. After months huddled around wells and seep holes, the natives disperse across the ephemeral ranges to graze their cattle amongst the tall grass springing miraculously from the sodden earth. But for Petherick the rainy season would always be the most dangerous in El Obeid, the air pernicious, impregnated with miasma rising from stagnant pools; a damp, penetrating south wind gnawing at the thread of life. One corner of the cemetery was reserved for Europeans who quicker than most succumbed to the degradation, despair, and disease.

Of all the town's horrors, the most feared was the 'hospital' in which Egyptian 'doctors' operated with rusty razor blades, their only experience trial and error. The sick stood a far better chance of curing themselves after their own fashion than in the 'house of slaughter' where their only hope was *Allah kerim* (God is merciful).[1] No European survived El Obeid longer than Petherick.

The town was no more than a cluster of small villages at the edge of a sandy plain, the houses of reed and straw held together by animal dung, except for those owned by prosperous Arab merchants. The *jallabas* – Sunni Muslim traders – built El Obeid at the end of the 18th century because of its proximity to the Nuba Mountains, for centuries a source of slaves, firstly for the Islamic Funj Kingdom of Sennar, then the Sultans of Darfur, and during Petherick's days, the Egyptians and Middle East Arabs. He arrived in the dry season, accompanied by his interpreter from the Eastern Desert Expedition, Ibrahim Effendi, and two soldiers assigned for their protection. The drifting sand lay waist deep round the mud huts; the town wrapped in a putrefying stench from the large holes into which corpses were thrown for dogs and hyenas to fight over. At first, the constant howling kept Petherick awake but in time he was as indifferent to it as the natives.[2]

Little is known about the five years the Welshman would eventually spend in El Obeid. The first visit was as a mining engineer employed by the Viceroy to explore for iron ore, the search for coal by then having been abandoned. When the Egyptian Government's monopoly of the gum arabic trade ended, he returned as a trader but said very little about this period, leaving a black hole that filled with rumour and suspicion. In his journal, these missing years were dismissed as unworthy of comment, covering as they did 'old ground', he said.[3] As regards slavery, although not denying it existed, Petherick was ambivalent and dispassionate, as if it were a ship that passed in the night. All the same, he did list the prices quoted by the slave traders in the market at El Obeid:

The prices of slaves in Kordofan, bordering as it does on Negro populations are so very low that few are without the means of acquiring them. A lad of fifteen or twenty years may be purchased for from £5 to £8, and a girl of the same age from £8 to £12; children from six to ten years of age, according to their sex and beauty, vary from £4 to £12. These are about the value of slaves when first introduced by the slave-merchants from their native hills; but domestic slaves when re-sold, fetch from half as much again to double the sums stated. A great number of slaves are reared in the families of the Kordofanese, by whom they are looked upon in nearly the same light as members, and very rarely are they sold, and then only in cases of great emergency.[4]

Slavery was 'in vogue', Petherick conceded but it was not until the final years of his seventeen in Egypt and the Sudan that he seriously challenged it. Petherick's account of the greater part of that period was sanitized for a genteel Victorian readership, peppered with lively descriptions of jolly scarf-clad natives of 'all shades, from the darkest ebony to the clear straw-colour of the Megrebbin, and the muddy white of the Egyptian fellah girl'. Contemporaries, however, were more graphic, in particular the Austrian Ignatius Pallme who visited Kordofan in 1837–1839. According to him, slaves were herded like cattle by auctioneers bawling out the prices – teeth, eyes, hands and feet all examined at the point of sale. 'The unfortunate wretch follows the crier like a dog, anxiously awaiting his fate. A mother may not be separated from the infant at her breast but [her] children of three or four years of age may be disposed of separately,' wrote Pallme.[5] There was even a three-day 'cooling off' period following transactions during which slaves could be returned to the vendor if found to have bad breath, snored, or were incontinent.

Children born into slavery were the property of the owner who, if he fathered a child by a slave, was permitted to sell his own offspring. The penalty for stealing a slave was the same as for stealing a cow: amputation of a hand by the local butcher, which took only a few minutes, the stump thrust into a pot of boiling butter to prevent haemorrhaging, then wrapped in a rag. 'In short,' wrote Pallme, 'whatever is considered most cruel and revolting by all civilized nations, is treated with the utmost levity in this country, so that it is, indeed, impossible to find words to give full vent to your feelings of indignation and horror.'

Pallme estimated 200,000 Black Africans from Central and East Africa were sold into slavery in 1839, and he firmly believed that 'several European journals' were conspiring in a cover up, observing acerbically: 'What right has Muhammad Ali [to be] called by many Europeans the civilizer of his country when we have ample proof of his forcing his people to steal slaves in order to satisfy his claims as Regent?'[6]

Pallme's account of the slave traffic in Kordofan during Petherick's residency was substantiated by Richard Holroyd in 1838, and again in 1847 by Mansfield Parkyns. Both were horrified by the heart-rending scenes, Holroyd describing a garrison returning to El Obeid from a razzia (slave hunt) in the Nuba Mountains:

These expeditions were called *ghaziyeh* and when I arrived at
El Obeid the troops had just returned with the produce of such an
expedition. The handsome women were sold for the harems of the
Turks and Arabs; the able-bodied men were placed in the ranks;
the decrepit, the pregnant females, and young children, were allotted to the soldiers in lieu of money [pay] ... A slave, therefore,
who had been received by two soldiers in lieu of 300 piastres was
sold in the bazaar for little more than half that sum; and more were
daily hawked about and disposed of by public auction.[7]

Mansfield Parkyns – whose path crossed Petherick's in 1847 – also wit-
nessed a *razzia*, in fact, helped finance it with a short-term loan to the
local governor Mustafa Pasha to help him fill a rush order from Cairo for
5,000 slaves.[8] Petherick's version of the same event was markedly different: not a slave hunt but a punishment raid against a band of renegade
Baggara Arabs. Thousands of cattle, not slaves were seized to pay the garrison, although Petherick admitted the troops promptly sold the cattle to
merchants for bartering to the Baggara for slaves and ivory.[9] Slaves were,
in effect, ready money, and passed from hand to hand.

But slavery was not wholly an Arab imposition. The natives had for
centuries routinely seized women and children as domestics, the men as
labourers while their owners lay in the shade. It was common for the
strongest to exchange the weakest members for food in time of famine.[10]
But unlike those enslaved by Arab and European traders, the chattel slaves
of African tribes did not generally suffer undue hardship. Prisoners taken
during tribal warfare if not executed were bartered. By renouncing his
personal freedom the native slave entered into a 'family' but this changed
for the worse with the arrival of Arab and European slave traders.[9]

Because they were regarded as docile and devoted, Black Africans
were highly esteemed, anthropologists remarking on their essentially
feminine characteristics, their soft voices, clear articulation, velvety skin
and rounded muscles. Although physically strong, they were often timid
and inquisitive, quick to love and quick to quarrel, delighting in abject
submission, sometimes sacrificing themselves for those who despised and
oppressed them.[10]

The slave caravans shuffling across the desert to the Nile must have
been familiar to Petherick: the heads of the captives locked in large forked
wooden branches (*sheba*) fixed by iron pins across the back of the neck,
the iron rings around the ankles permitting but one step at a time; small
children manacled and towed like human daisy chains. The old and infirm

were beaten with the butt-end of muskets if they faltered. Those unable to walk were dragged through the dust by a rope attached to the saddle-bow of a camel. Prayers and entreaties were of no avail. Wives were torn from their husbands, and children from their mothers. The exhausted were abandoned without a drop of water to relieve their final hours. The few who did escape urinated on their fetters to corrode the iron.[11]

It may be that Petherick's pragmatism was influenced by the view prevailing among sections of British society that the slavery issue was settled by the ending of the Triangular Trade, leaving the Royal Navy to mop up the remaining pockets of illegal activity. The impression that the struggle was over was echoed by the *Times* which advised the British Anti-Slavery Society to find itself 'a new name and occupation':

> Considering that we utterly abolished slavery in our dominions twenty years ago, that we paid £20 million [compensation to Caribbean plantation owners] to do it handsomely and have spent £500,000 a year to keeping the work weather-tight ever since, it might be thought fairly enough that we had done with the business and that our estimable philanthropists might turn their energies into some of the many channels which could find them fresh employment. As the most zealous sympathizers can now find little ground for complaint on behalf of native Africans – the most carefully protected race under the sun – the solicitude of the Society is transferred to the Coolies of southern India and to the migratory population of China ... as if slavery had never been abolished at all. A free black in the West Indies can now enjoy existence with fewer of its obligations than any other specimen of man known to ethnologists ... why cannot the Anti-Slavery Society be satisfied with so triumphant a result?[12]

But did Petherick's pragmatism become indifference, hiding a darker side to the 'missing' years in El Obeid? On occasion, the Welshman's ambivalence sounded like an apology for the Egyptian Government. Had not the 'Viceroy Said Pasha (1854–1863) done much to check the trade by preventing the public sale of slaves and liberating all who complained of ill-treatment?' he wrote.[13] Not really! Public slave markets in Khartoum, Cairo, and Alexandria may have been prohibited to avoid offending European sensibilities but the trade continued to flourish at various places along the Nile, even in the suburbs of Cairo behind closed doors. Another assertion that Muhammad Ali Pasha had abolished slavery in 1847 by terminating the recruitment of black slaves as soldiers was also untrue. Some years later, the Viceroy's successor Said Pasha rounded up several hundred Black Africans from the Nuba Mountains to serve as bodyguards!

Petherick's return to El Obeid in 1849 when his contract ended following the death of the Viceroy was at the suggestion of the British Consul-General in Egypt, Charles Murray, who saw the termination of the gum arabic monopoly as a business opportunity for Britain. For Petherick the quid pro quo was his appointment as Vice-Consul for the Sudan, Murray having decided official British representation was advisable after the Austrian Government appointed a consular agent. Writing to the Foreign Secretary, Lord Palmerston, Murray said it was absolutely essential that British subjects engaged in the gum trade – Petherick was then the only one – should be protected 'against the rapacity of the [Egyptian] Government who are constantly in the habit of seizing goods and extorting illegal payments':

> The person I would recommend to Your Lordship to fill this post is Mr John Petherick whom I think well qualified to fill it for the following reasons: he is by profession a mining engineer which is sufficient guarantee for his education and requirements. He is also well skilled in geology and would be found very useful in producing any scientific investigations which Her Majesty's Government might hereafter desire to have made in those interesting and undeveloped regions. Mr Petherick has also the advantage of speaking Arabic fluently and he writes and reads it sufficiently for the transaction of ordinary business, so that he could have no need of a Dragoman [interpreter, official guide] to carry on his intercourse either with the Governor or the natives.
>
> As his object in visiting these regions is to trade in their produce, the influences and protection assured to him by his official charge, would be sufficient inducement for him to accept it without any salary from Her Majesty's Government, but I would suggest to Your Lordship that he might be allowed the wages of one Turkish Janissary [beadle or usher]. These would amount only to ten dollars a month or twenty-one Pounds a year, and the assistance of such a functionary would be of great use to him in his intercourse with the local authorities or on detached service in according protection to British travellers and traders at Dongola, Kordofan or other points distant from his post.[14]

As it happened, Petherick spoke only pidgin Arabic, and never wrote it. Significantly, Murray does not mention the slave trade; certainly not Petherick's responsibilities with regard to suppressing it. Britain's interests in Egypt and the Sudan were entirely commercial, gum arabic then, as it is today, a valuable commodity widely used in the food processing, pharmaceutical, and paint industries. Although the appointment was unpaid, Petherick's superior status gave him leverage over commercial rivals mostly represented by lesser powers such as Tuscany, Sardinia, Greece, and Naples whose consular agents were also traders, intent on exploiting their position to advance their own interests. Ignorant of consular duties, and with no sense of dignity, they would have embarrassed home governments were they not on the remote fringes of the known world. The Sardinian Vice-Consul Alexandre Vaudey was a violent criminal who was dismissed only to be replaced by M. Antoine Brun-Rollet, a noted slave trader whose sole qualification was that he was the only Sardinian available. Petherick's qualification was no different: he was the only British subject in Sudan, apart from three related Maltese families – de Bono, Miceli and Mussu – and one Levantine under British protection. But the appointment added a veneer of respectability to the man described as a 'John Bull' character, brash and aggressive – an early-day imperialist grasping at every opportunity to carve out a hard living in a hard school.

During the whole of Petherick's five years in the gum arabic trade there were never more than two or three permanent European residents in El Obeid. One was the zoologist (and future French Vice-Consul) George Thibaut, remembered for supplying giraffes to London's Regent's Park Zoo; another the self-styled French 'Count', Alphonse de Malzac, a notorious slave trader, business associate and 'close friend' of Petherick. The only rule the expatriates observed was that no one asked about the past, de Malzac claiming to be a former French diplomat, while another French adventurer, M. J. A. Vayssiere, styled himself lieutenant in the Chasseurs D'Afrique in Algeria when, in fact, he was only ever an army conscript.

With fewer than twenty Europeans resident in the Sudan and Kordofan at one time, Petherick's choice of associates was inevitably restricted. But claiming a 'lasting friendship' with de Malzac and the slave-hunting Governor of El Obeid, Mustafa Pasha, were self-inflicted wounds. A 'good, kind-hearted man … a distinguished host …' he wrote of the Governor. Six feet tall, in the prime of life, and clean-shaven with a black moustache curling upwards from the corners of his mouth, the Governor according to Petherick was 'good natured, jovial but stern and honest', a man whose friendship he valued. No mention was made of the *razzias* or the daily slave markets the Governor presided over.[15]

Whatever the reputational damage caused by socializing with rogues and ruffians, Petherick's excursion into the gum trade proved highly profitable until the market was undermined by cheaper gum from West Africa. Casting around for another commodity to exploit, it was perhaps inevitable he chose ivory, more valuable than gum and from what he discovered on an expedition to Darfur, more plentiful. His search for new sources of gum arabic took him three hundred miles west of El Obeid to El Fasher in Darfur, an independent Black African Islamic sultanate until 1916 when it was seized by the British and incorporated into the Sudan. Bounded by the Sahara in the north, Chad in the west, and the Sudanese province of Bahr al-Ghazal in the south west, Darfur was seldom visited by outsiders. In 1792 the Englishman William Browne was the first European to enter this largely unknown kingdom the size of Spain. Petherick was the first to return after the Sultan believing Browne to be an Egyptian 'spy' held him prisoner for three years. The indigenous Fur people were suspicious of strangers, believing Egypt had designs on their arid plain and volcanic mountain range!

Any expedition to Darfur was approached with the utmost caution. Mansfield Parkyns who passed through El Obeid in 1847 carrying a firman from the Viceroy discovered it ran out at the border with Darfur. After a year of planning, Parkyns finally abandoned the idea as too dangerous and returned to England.

Evidently, Petherick had no such concerns, his search for gum arabic leading him ever deeper into Darfur's sandy wilderness, to within a hundred miles of the present-day Chad border. But there were no international boundaries in mid-19th century Africa, only tribal areas. Even these homelands were confusing, depending from whom the traveller obtained directions. Petherick was the first European to encounter the Niam-Niam, at one time inhabiting an area extending from Lake Chad to the Nile's confluence with the Sobat River, and south as far as the equator. Niam-Niam were supposedly cannibalistic although Petherick only ever heard the stories but never saw the evidence. More confusing was that Niam-Niam was a Dinka name, and the Dinkas and the Nuer were the predominant tribes further south, together with two smaller, possibly sub-groups, the Jur and Bongo. The Dinka were also found along the White Nile's eastern bank in what was generally regarded as Shillook territory. The Aazande straddling the Congo-Nile watershed were often known to early explorers as Niam-Niam.[16]

Petherick's final visit to Dafur before moving to Khartoum to trade ivory was in 1853. The 'capital' El Fasher was a few hundred mud huts scattered across a dusty slope, and its sheikh, Ismain Wallad Minaim, a trading

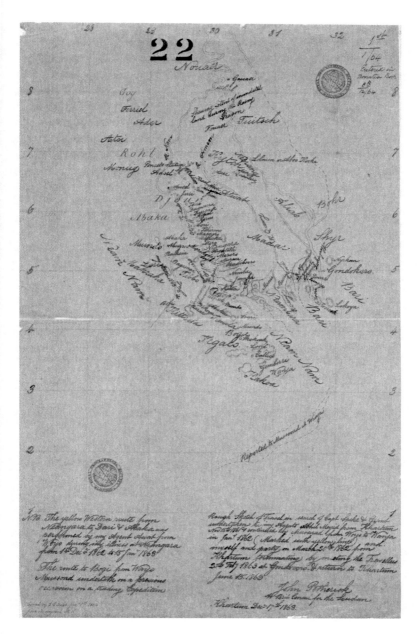

Figure 10. *Petherick's rough sketch map showing the separate routes taken by himself and Speke/Grant to Gondokoro in 1863.*

partner whose slaves harvested gum arabic for sale to the Welshman. The Sheikh, an 'excessively good natured man with unbounded hospitality, and love of *araki*' was waiting behind a thorny barricade to greet his friend.

'After tiring out each other's patience with endless pattings of the palms of our right hands, and repetitions of the word taibeen ('Are you well?' or 'How are you?'),' recalled Petherick, 'we were conducted to the centre of the yard, to a spacious *rakuba* where we found a numerous party of Arabs squatted on the sand, its floor. In lieu of coffee we were helped to *merissa*.' [17]

After being provided with fresh camels by the Sheikh, Petherick headed south to explore a hitherto unknown region – the Bahr al-Ghazal river basin, a vast swampland during the wet season but in the dry a prairie of vivid green grass stretching to the far horizon like a boundless field of corn teeming with game. Petherick had found an apparently inexhaustible source of ivory some elephant herds over five hundred strong.

The Bahr al-Ghazal was depicted in the popular Victorian literature of the period as a land of pygmies, swamps and forests inhabited by cannibals. Draining an area the size of the United Kingdom, its streams and rivers flow off the Nile-Congo watershed into the river of the same name to become the White Nile's largest tributary. The river entrance was often blocked by floating vegetation but beyond these dams stretched a thousand miles of navigable waterways allowing Petherick access to some of Africa's most profitable elephant grounds. Determined to capitalise upon the discovery, Petherick packed his bags and headed for Khartoum. The rainy season was at its height, the desert criss-crossed by streams 'running through wooded glens' reminding him of 'the brooks amongst my native hills of fair Glamorgan'.[18]

CHAPTER 4

Khartoum, Ivory and Slaves

WHEREAS PRACTICALLY LITTLE IS KNOWN about the five 'missing' years in El Obeid – other than Petherick's assertion they were devoted entirely to harvesting gum – his movements are more clear when he establishes himself as an ivory trader in Khartoum. At first he lived in a baked-mud hut on the banks of the Blue Nile, ideal during the winter when exposed to fresh north winds, but in summer damp and unhealthy, Petherick suffering his first attack of malaria. A cold fit set his teeth chattering, followed by hot, dry shivers, a blinding headache and delirium. Utterly exhausted he lay on his bed for weeks, dosing himself with quinine until advised by a doctor to move to higher ground. Only when the colder winds blew from the north again did Petherick recover.

Khartoum at the junction of the Blue and White Niles was a miserable, filthy and unhealthy place, not very different from El Obeid but much larger. Twenty thousand people lived in crude single storey buildings of sun-dried bricks, the Roman Catholic Mission the only one built of stone. Dead animals rotted in the streets; torture and flogging were regular occurrences. The heat was always overwhelming, and when the wind blew the sand-filled sky turned as black as night. Samuel Baker, explorer and big game hunter, wrote:

> I saw approaching from the south west apparently, a solid range of immense brown mountains high in the air. So rapid was the approach of this extraordinary phenomenon that in a few minutes we were in actual pitch darkness. At first there was no wind, and the peculiar calm gave an oppressive character to the event ... We tried to distinguish our hands placed close before our eyes – not even an outline could be seen. This lasted for upwards of twenty minutes; it then rapidly passed away and the sun shone as before.[1]

Khartoum was a melting pot for fortune-seekers, and those fleeing Egyptian jurisdiction. If it were not for the slave trade it would not have existed, an estimated 40,000 passing through the town every year during the 1850s. Colourful sailing barges crowded the riverbanks; caravans from the heart of Africa threaded their way through the town with exotic animals, birds, and plants not previously known to civilisation. According to Baker, however, Khartoum was also about kidnap and murder. The amount of legitimate trade including ivory was a 'mere bagatelle' compared to the profits from slave trafficking on the Nile, in which Europeans were also engaged, Baker providing a graphic account of slaving activities during Petherick's residency:

> Throughout the Sudan money is exceedingly scarce and the rate of interest exorbitant ... varying from thirty-six to eighty per cent. So high a rate deters all honest enterprise ... The wild speculator borrows upon such terms, to rise suddenly like a rocket, or to fall like its exhausted stick. Thus, honest enterprise being impossible, dishonesty takes the lead, and a successful expedition to the White Nile is supposed to overcome all charges. A man without means borrows money ... hires several vessels and engages from 100 to 300 men, composed of Arabs and runaway villains from distant countries ... he purchases guns ... together with a few hundred pounds of beads. The vessels sail about December and on arrival at the desired locality they proceed into the interior until they arrive ... quietly surrounding the village while its occupants sleep. They fire the grass, pour volleys of musketry through the flaming thatch ... panic-stricken the men are shot down like pheasants ... the women and children kidnapped ... and fastened by their necks in a living chain ... boats packed with human cargo are landed a few days from Khartoum at which places agents, or purchasers wait ... for the most part Arabs.[2]

The rewards were considerable for those gambling with their lives. Their greatest obstacle was the Sudd, a vast swamp straddling the White Nile which had for centuries prevented traders from reaching Gondokoro, then the furthest navigable point on the river – and gateway to the hunting grounds for slaves and ivory. Not until an Egyptian Government Expedition broke through the swamp in 1846 did Khartoum traders start moving south. Before that the trade route was from Zanzibar on the East African coast inland as far as lakes Nyasa, Victoria, and Tanganyika.

Petherick's interest in the Nile was essentially commercial. Unlike his British contemporaries the Welshman was no blue-eyed man of destiny driven by a burning ambition to see over the next hill, to plant the Union flag across Central Africa's unexplored heartlands. His sights were fixed on elephants, his geographic discoveries – although of huge significance – incidental to his real business.

This is not to say Petherick was a stranger to triumphalist imperialism. The Union flag flying from the mastheads of his Nile fleet or from the point of a lance when advancing through the interior was to wave in the faces of commercial rivals, but not as a banner in the scramble for Africa. To tap the most profitable sources of ivory Petherick established a chain of trading stations (*zaribas*) first along the Bahr al-Ghazal and Sobat tributaries of the Nile, then on the Congo/Nile watershed and, finally, close to the equator where tusks, reputedly, lay thick on the ground. Driven by the profit motive, Petherick the ivory trader penetrated deep into the unknown regions of Central Africa long before the arrival of Livingstone and the Welsh-American Henry Morton Stanley.

The Welshman knew about ivory, in particular the difference between hard and soft, the Congo border the dividing line between the two. West of this it was hard, glossy, heavier, and more difficult to carve. To the east of the line the softer ivory was white, opaque, smooth, gently curved, easily worked, and consequently more valuable. Buyers said the best came from the drier, upland regions where it was so plentiful the natives used it for fence posts. The further into the interior Petherick pressed the more incredulous the natives seemed about his offer to exchange valuable glass beads for useless tusks of elephants. At one village, in which they spoke of eating their old and infirm as well as runaway slaves, the entire population set off to gather discarded ivory, returning at the end of the day with tusks each weighing several hundredweight but mostly degraded, having been exposed to the weather for too long. 'I managed to explain that the tusks I required must be uninjured and smooth, like those of an elephant I killed the day before,' said Petherick. 'For a moment they were disappointed [but] soon gave way to rejoicing, and entreated [me] that if we would remain until the moon became small, the elephants would come, and they would kill every one possessed of tusks in their own way.'

After a fortnight, the beat of tom-toms announced the approach of a herd of eighteen elephants, every 'old man, hag, warrior, woman and child' accompanied by slaves forming a vast circle around the herd. The bush was set alight engulfing the animals in the roar and crackle of flames. When the smoke cleared, the natives swooped upon the petrified beasts with barbed lances. 'The sight was grand,' recalled Petherick, 'and although their tusks proved a rich prize I was touched at the massacre.' It took two days for the villagers to cut up the carcasses, and another two to barter, every purchase watched by a crowd of excited natives, standing in a tight circle around the mountain of ivory because although sales were controlled by the tribal chief some tusks were owned by several persons. After a long and tiresome process, his stock of coloured beads exhausted, Petherick had among his purchases one tusk taller than any man at 7 feet 2 inches long and weighing 185 lbs. After the tusk was cut out with a steel axe, another two feet remained buried in the elephant's skull.[4] But finding a perfect pair was difficult, one usually more worn than the other having been used to tear up small trees.[3]

Besides the differences in quality, the ivory trader needed to be aware of the changing fashions among the natives because blue beads exchanged for ivory one year might not be in demand the next. Some merchants were seriously out of pocket after arriving in the interior with the wrong colour beads! But such occasions were rare. The 19th century story from Central Africa was that fabulous riches awaited the brave; that some traders returning from the interior needed 2,000 porters to carry the spoils. Natives were expected to bear staggering weights, one porter, according to the missionary David Livingstone, humping 200 lbs of ivory on his head from the Central African lakes region to the coast at Zanzibar, more than 700 miles.[4]

Most Europeans were lured to the Sudan by the prospect of making a quick fortune. One of these, an Italian from Lucca, Adolfo Antognoli, explained to a friend:

> I am going to try and make money or have my belly ripped open by Blacks. Take my word for it; for a young man it's a marvellous investment for, with 2–3,000 dollars' worth of goods, a man can make 10–12,000. Sure, you must risk all to gain all. But if you make three or four voyages [up the White Nile], you will become a man of substance, a little gentleman …[5]

When Petherick arrived in Khartoum in 1853 one hundred tons of ivory was being shipped down the Nile every year, a pound of beads buying him 10 lbs of ivory. He estimated the trade to be worth £40,000 a year – or £2.5m at 2005 prices.[6] By 1859 as the elephant herds closest to the White Nile were depleted, beads and ivory were, weight for weight, worth the same – and slaves became more profitable for the unscrupulous.

Figure 11. *(opposite)* *The Sudd and the White Nile basin.*

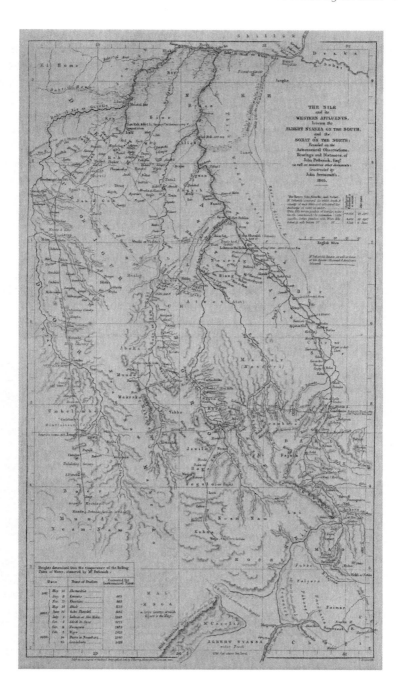

For some Khartoum traders, *zaribas* were not trading stations but fortresses in the forest protected by thorn barricades from behind which mercenaries were deployed to raid surrounding villages for cattle to trade for ivory at the rate of one cow for a large tusk. Women and children taken during *razzias* were ransomed for ivory until their value as slaves became greater. Alliances were struck between armed mercenaries and local tribes to incite tribal warfare as a means of seizing more cattle to trade for slaves. Not surprisingly, the hostility of the indigenous peoples intensified when those hired as porters to deliver tusks to boats waiting on the Nile never returned. Instead of being paid in beads, pieces of cloth, copper, and brass, they were sold.[7]

Petherick never ventured south without his own private 'army'. According to him, the slave trade on the White Nile was driven by Egyptians, Italians and Greeks who together employed 15,000 men in human trafficking, one merchant – Agad and Company – having sole trading rights over a territory half the size of France. Strangely, not once did Petherick report this explosion in the slave trade to the Foreign Office, his diplomatic career remarkable only for what he never did during his ten

Figure 12. *Cattle swim the Nile at the beginning of the Sudd swamp somewhere below Lake No, driven by natives in dugout canoes.*

Figure 13. *Nuer porters cross the Sudd carrying loads on their heads.*

years as Vice-Consul in the Sudan from 1849–1859. What little is known of his interventions on behalf of the British Government suggests he was neither busy with diplomacy, nor very good at it when obliged to act. So few were his consular duties he was rarely mentioned in Foreign Office dispatches prior to 1859. The first occasion concerned a quarrel between Andrea de Bono, doyen of the Maltese clan – and as such a British subject – and a Turk over a consignment of ivory. The latter had threatened to cut off de Bono's head, wrap it in the Union Jack and feed it to the crocodiles.

Significantly, the second mention was a sharp reprimand from the Foreign Office for involving himself in Islamic chattel slavery by attempting to release three slave girls accused of stealing from their employer. But he did ask the Consul-General in Alexandria to support his application to the Egyptian Government to import twenty-five muskets for protection. Such ambivalence towards the slave trade, with which he rubbed shoulders at every twist and turn of the Nile, might be at least partially explained by the failure of the Foreign Office to issue him with any instructions for dealing with it. Then there was the remoteness. No member of the British diplomatic mission in Alexandria had ever visited the Sudan, a dispatch between the two places taking at least six weeks, and a reply just as long. Petherick spent many months in the interior travelling between

Figure 14. *Nuer youths with spears and shields hunting hippopotamus in one of the Sudd's many papyrus-filled lagoons.*

Figure 15. *Dinka tribesmen at a funeral dance.*

various trading stations when his only means of communication was by native runner.

Of the seven *zaribas* Petherick had, five can be located. The one at Gaba-Shambyl (between 5° and 8° North) in the Bahr al-Ghazal was shared with his 'highly valued friend' Alphonse de Malzac; another was at the mouth of the Sobat River; one at Wayo west of the White Nile towards the Congo border; and Mundo was among the reputedly cannibalistic Niam-Niam. Petherick's most southerly station, and closest to the equator was at Falaro (3° 40' N), among one of the most hostile of Central African tribes, the Bari. At Falaro he was in partnership with the Maltese Amabile de Bono, nephew of Andrea de Bono who by the age of nineteen was already a notorious slave trader. All Petherick's stations were garrisoned, that at Falaro by a hundred 'adventurers without a home … of every Egyptian caste and colour'. Most were located in lawless areas outside the reach of Egyptian jurisdiction – beyond the White Nile's great natural barrier: the Sudd, the disease-ridden swamp larger than Wales which had frustrated all attempts by traders and explorers to reach the interior.

The ancients were intrigued by what lay beyond the Sudd, an area now embracing the independent countries of Rwanda, Burundi, Uganda, the Republic of South Sudan, and the Democratic Republic of Congo. In the 5th century BC the Greek Herodotus placed the source of the Nile among the mysterious Mountains of the Moon. But he rejected the notion that Egypt's life-sustaining annual flood was the result of snow melting on the mountains because of the widely held belief that the equator was the Torrid Zone where humans were devoured by ferocious animals. How, he asked, could there be snow in such a place?

The twin arms of the 4,130-mile (6,656 kilometres) river, the Blue and White Niles become one at Khartoum, the Blue Nile flowing westwards out of the Ethiopian Highlands providing the bulk of the flood waters and alluvial deposits without which Egypt would not exist. The Scottish explorer James Bruce had mapped the Blue Nile from its source at Lake Tana (12° 02' 09" N, 037° 15' 53" E; 12.03583° N, 37.26472° E) to Khartoum in 1780.

The White Nile's river system south of Khartoum is complex, covering a vast area, in the process draining a tenth of Africa. By the early nineteenth century attempts to reach the source of the Nile usually ended at the euphemistically named Lake No (9° 29' 52" N, 30° 7' 54" E), in effect a lagoon at the juncture of the Bahr al-Jabal (the Mountain Nile) and its longest tributary the Bahr al-Ghazal. By the time it reaches Lake No, the Mountain Nile has lost 50 per cent of its water in the enormous papyrus-choked swamp, the Sudd – meaning 'block' in Arabic. At one time it was thought that the Bahr al-Ghazal draining the Congo Basin was the more likely source of the Nile. Petherick thought so and was the first European to navigate its 425 miles (683 kilometres). The Mountain Nile was invariably blocked by thick mats of floating vegetation where it crossed the Sudd (5°–10° North). In the wet season from July to November, 6,000 square miles (16,000 square kilometres) flooded, creating a bewildering series of lakes and floating aquatic islands, the matted vegetation often dense enough to walk upon as the river meandered through a huge pestilential swamp of papyrus as tall as sugar cane. The heat was relentless, mosquitoes ('Nile nightingales') creeping into every aperture. Without landmarks and boundaries, the Sudd was according to Petherick a timeless space filled with melancholy and putrid vegetation, as infectious as an open sewer. When the wind blew the channel was lost amongst the drifting vegetation. When it didn't Petherick sent his men into the putrid soup to fasten ropes to the tall grass so that his boat could be dragged against the current. Petherick's usual approach to the Sudd was to drive his sailing barge at maximum speed into the most elastic part of the barrier to prise open a channel while his crew ripped away the stinking vegetation with forked poles. When this failed the barrier was set alight. Quite often the only way to force a passage was to tear the whole mass apart piece by piece, a process that could take several weeks. Every day they were drenched by rain. At sunset a cold dense fog arose from the river and hung over the boat. Sleep was impossible, the hours passed in semi-stupor swimming in a vapour bath. In the morning, Petherick's bed was covered with thousands of mosquitoes crushed as he tossed and turned. When he ate, a servant stood at his side waving an ostrich feather fan to drive the tormenting insects off his food and from his mouth.

Nor did the Sudd improve with time. Twenty years after Petherick crossed it regularly in a sailing barge another explorer, Dr E.W. Felkiu, travelling by Nile steamer, recalled:

The river was dark and dirty. Supposing you called for a glass of water, you obtained a liquid mixture of mud and water; if a pinch of alum was added to clear it, the result was that about a quarter of an inch of mud was deposited at the bottom of the glass.

... Now and then dead fish floated past, and at times the decaying body of a native was slowly borne down the stream. The air was alive with mosquitoes, whose attacks continued by day as well as by night. More than half the crew was down with fever.[8]

But the blanket of choking vegetation served a purpose, and still does by preventing greater evaporation which would reduce the water supply reaching Lower Egypt.

The first recorded expedition sent by the Roman Emperor Nero in AD 66 failed to get further than the Sudd. Using this and other sources, the Alexandria-based Greek scholar and geographer Claudius Ptolemy (AD 90–AD 118) placed the source of the Blue and White Niles as twin lakes near the equator. In his *Geographia*, Ptolemy drew upon the work of an earlier geographer, Marinos of Tyre, as well as on Roman and Persian gazetteers. In addition, he cited the Greek merchant Diogenes and other travellers who claimed to have journeyed inland from the coast of East Africa and looked upon two great lakes and snowy mountains. Diogenes may have come upon either Lake Nyassa or Lake Victoria (or both) while the snow-capped mountains in the distance were almost certainly the Rwenzori range along the boundary between today's Uganda and the Democratic Republic of the Congo. This view prevailed into the 18th century when Guillaume de L'Isle (1675–1726), the father of modern geography discarded the lakes theory as the source of the Blue and White Niles. While his map, 'L'Afrique dressée sur les observations de Ms. de l'Academie Royale des Sciences' (1700) correctly showed the headwaters of the Blue Nile as Lake Tana in Abyssinia (Ethiopia), the source of the White Nile remained a mystery. Later cartographers repositioned the mountains and the lakes further south – where they remained until 1859 when the Rwenzori range was identified as Ptolemy's snow-capped Mountains of the Moon rising to 16,000 feet between Lake Albert and Lake Edward.

The Sudd was eventually crossed in 1840 by Salim Qapudan, a Circassian sent by the Viceroy Muhammad Ali Pasha to search for gold. After two months and 750 miles, the expedition struggled into Gondokoro (4° 49' 30.61" N, 31° 36' 38.94" E), decimated by disease and hostile natives. Salim had, however, lifted the curtain on Central Africa's great potential: its abundance of ivory, gold, copper, iron, and slaves traded for handfuls of coloured beads and strips of calico. The Frenchman George d'Arnaud who accompanied Salim's expedition, afterwards drew the first more or less accurate map, showing the river's course as far as Gondokoro beyond which further navigation was blocked by seventy miles of rapids.[9]

The first British attempt to reach the interior and the source of the Nile was in 1857 by Captain Richard Burton, accompanied by Captain John Hanning Speke, the explorers heading inland to the lakes region from Zanzibar on Africa's east coast. After leaving his fever-stricken companion Burton resting on the banks of Lake Tanganyika, Speke pushed north

and in July 1858 become the first European to set eyes upon the mighty
Victoria Nyanza. Hurrying home, his rush to publicise the discovery and
deny Burton a share of the credit triggered a monumental quarrel in which
John Petherick would become embroiled when the Royal Geographical
Society sent Speke back to Africa to take a closer look at Victoria Nyanza –
the inland 'sea' whose southern shore he had only briefly seen.

CHAPTER 5

Exploration and Trade

ETHERICK'S FIRST ATTEMPT AT BREAKING THROUGH the
swamp ended in failure. The sailing barges bound for Gondokoro
headed south from Khartoum when the wind blew from the north
in autumn. On 19 November 1853, Petherick's dahabeeyah (small dhow)
was one of twenty that left the river port loaded with mercenaries recruited
from Khartoum's slums and destined for the *zaribas*, some to trade legiti-
mately, others to raid and plunder. Gondokoro was the main transit port
for slaves driven overland to the river from *zaribas*, fortified clearings in
the African bush where they were imprisoned after being seized deep in
the equatorial forest. Petherick had told Murray, Consul-General, that he
was heading south to hunt elephants in 1851. There is no record that he
did until two years later when he left with several tons of glass beads,
cowry shells and a variety of 'trifles' to batter for ivory.[1] The crew had a
rousing send-off as, protected by twenty armed Arab mercenaries, the sails
of the dahabeeyah caught the north wind lashing the river's surface into
long curling waves.

Crouching in the bows, Petherick amused himself with potshots at the
crocodiles basking at the river's edge before turning his gun on the flocks
of Nile geese scattering across their path as the barge sailed slowly between
islands of mimosa grazed by herds of shaggy, black goats. After each crack
of the rifle a member of the crew, ignoring the crocodiles, jumped in to fish
out their evening meal.

At latitude 13.75° North the dahabeeyah passed the last Egyptian settlement, watched from a sand bar by two tall naked Shillook warriors lean-
ing on spears, small blue monkeys playing at their feet and antelopes and
gazelles diving for cover. The Welshman had crossed into an unknown,
savage world; the smoke curling above the tree tops a warning that it
wasn't as deserted as it seemed. Quite suddenly, a group of naked Baggara

Arab horsemen rode down to the river's edge, hurling insults as the boat drifted up stream on the breeze. A single shot dispersed the riders preying upon the Dinkas living along the river's edge. But next morning they were back with five Dinka child captives for sale to Arab slave traders.[2]

When the breeze died and the sails hung limp, Petherick left the crew to drag the heavy barge upstream, buckled a pair of Dean and Adams double-action revolvers around his waist, and after picking up an elephant gun jumped ashore. Spotting a troop of giraffes browsing the treetops, he removed his boots and crawled silently to within range of a dark-brown bull:

> A well-placed shoulder shot made him reel and bound and after a couple of hundred yards galloping like a rocking horse he came down in an avalanche. The report of my rifle and my own mad antics soon brought up my men, and never was there such rejoicing. More men were sent for, and it was late in the afternoon before the animal appeared in fragments on board. A good supper and a few bottles of *arrachi* produced the *tarabooka* and dancing. The height of good humour reigned until nightfall when, a breeze springing up, we were again moving under canvas.[3]

The next morning the shout 'elephant' brought him bounding on to the roof of the cabin. A magnificent Nile elephant, ears thrust forward, was charging the boat until halted in its tracks by a shot above the right eye. The animal turned and trotted off into the river before disappearing up the opposite bank, depriving Petherick of 'as fine a pair of tusks as ever a sportsman envied.'

Eight days after leaving Khartoum they reached Kaka, a slave market, and the most important of the Shillook villages, the natives a 'fine, tall, and well-made race, perfectly black with short woolly hair ... good-looking if it were not for the disfiguration caused by the extraction of the four lower front teeth'. Both sexes were completely naked, apart from married women who wore ankle-length hides front and back with 'bells at the bottom to prevent the wind taking too great a liberty'. At their next stop on the river Petherick bought ivory from a chief with fifteen wives and 73 children after the wives were permitted to examine his skin, hair and clothes.

At Latitude 10° N they passed the mouth of the Sobat River, the first of the White Nile's large tributaries. From there the river turned westwards into Lake No at the confluence with the Bahr al-Ghazal, and then south again into the Sudd, the passage through the swampland erratic and difficult to follow.

After Lake No's watery maze the dahabeeyah moored beside a Nuer village at Kyt, a long, low island covered in tall grass and reeds, the native cattle 'bolting like Welsh sheep'. Astonished by the sight of a white man, the natives were nonetheless friendly once Petherick accepted their peculiar welcome – the chief springing aboard, snatching his hand and spitting on the palm!

'Staggered at the man's audacity, my first impulse was to knock him down,' recalled Petherick. 'But his features expressing kindness only, I vented my rage by returning the compliment with all possible interest. His delight seemed excessive and, resuming his seat, he expressed to his companions his conviction that I must be a great chief.' The tribe had no ivory but for eight pigeon-egg-size beads they bought fresh milk and a bullock.

Lake No was explored as far as its juncture with the Bahr al-Ghazal, the dahabeeyah unable to proceed more than a few miles upstream. Turning back into the labyrinth, they floated aimlessly until a native fisherman guided them to what was thought to be a safe landing place. But waiting on the riverbank were hundreds of hostile savages waving clubs and lances, daring the strangers to step ashore. Arming himself, Petherick was all for forcing a landing but his men refused to follow, leaving no alternative but to retreat across Lake No to the mouth of the Sobat River where Petherick established his first trading station, leaving behind a dozen armed men to barter with the natives while he returned to Khartoum.[4]

In October the following year Petherick disembarked a much larger force on Kyt Island and, accompanied by eighty porters, headed southwest into the previously unexplored Bahr al-Ghazal tribal area. But instead of trading ivory, he and his men were seized, Petherick suspected for their baskets of coloured beads. The natives were more interested, however, in his back issue of the *Weekly Times* which Petherick read in the shade of a tree studying, so they thought, the little black dots on the paper! Was he the rainmaker they were expecting? The tribe and its cattle had been decimated by a long drought, and the stranger would not be allowed to leave until he made rain. When a demonstration of the White Man's firepower, coupled with his threat to sack the village, failed to break the impasse, Petherick strode fearlessly into their midst:

Seating myself in the centre of them opposite to the sub-chief, a man fully six feet six inches high, and proportionately well-made, I stated that no intimidation could produce rain ... that if I liked with one single discharge of my gun I could destroy the whole tribe and their cattle in an instant; but that with regard to rain, I would consult my oracle, and invited him [sub-chief] to appear with the whole of the tribe on the morrow, when they could hear the result.

The next morning the tribe assembled for the oracle's pronouncement.[5] Petherick held up a bottle filled with horse flies sprinkled with flour. The oracle had told him to liberate the flies, he said. If they were all recaptured it would rain but if only one fly escaped the drought would continue. Hundreds of clubs and lances were raised in the air, accompanied by shouts of 'Let them go ... let them go', at which point, muttering a prayer for the safety of the flies he smashed the bottle against the barrel of his rifle. Every man, woman and child set off in hot pursuit, struggling back at sunset exhausted, and with only two flour-coated flies. The ruse bought time: time for the return of a hunting party a few days later loaded with tusks bought from a neighbouring tribe. On seeing their mortal enemies consorting with the White magician, the natives consented to carry the ivory back to the river and boats. A contingent of Khartoumers remained behind to build another trading station and stockpile tusks for Petherick's return the following year.

After seven months in the interior, and with the river current in its favour and the wind at its back, Petherick's dahabeeyah made it to Khartoum ahead of the rainy season, but not before being attacked by hippopotami, five of the monsters attempting to clamber aboard. Most were sunk by Petherick's fusillade and their carcasses lost in the river, except for one caught in the shallows and butchered. But the hippopotami had their revenge – the cook. Sitting on the gun whale, his back to the river, the poor man was snatched off the deck and crushed between enormous jaws.[6]

Although Petherick complained that neither of these expeditions produced a profit he was soon planning another to collect tusks stockpiled at his various river stations while he led an even larger private 'army' further south. In a good season, a party of 150 men brought back 20,000 lbs of ivory worth £180,000 at 2005 prices. Ivory would soon prove especially lucrative for Petherick – more so, he always insisted, than slaves ever could be. So successful was he at finding elephants, his rivals were never very far behind. But the focus of the White Nile trade was changing, slaves proving easier to 'harvest' than ivory. Traders were also able to pay off their mercenaries in slaves, retaining the surplus for themselves – sometimes 400–500, worth £5–£6 each.[7]

Petherick was accused of being one of these slave traders by no other than his diplomatic colleague Dr Josef Natterer, the Austrian Vice-Consul in Khartoum. In April 1860 the Foreign Office received a translation of a report Natterer submitted to his Consul-General in Alexandria describing the whole European trading community on the White Nile as brigands, murderers, and slave traffickers. Although not mentioned by name, Petherick was by insinuation, and the Foreign Office asked for his comments. The allegations, he said, were all part of a covert attempt by the Austrian Government to colonize Central Africa, a response that was wholly misinformed and undiplomatic. The Natterer indictment remained on file to be used later as evidence of Petherick's involvement in the slave trade. The original report has been lost but the Austrian State Archives in Vienna has a copy in German, as well as the French translation sent to the British Foreign Office. This states that while no German or Austrian citizens were engaged in slaving, French traders, one Englishman, and one Maltese were trafficking: 'de toute le colonie de Khartoum il n'y a que les Francais, et de plus un Anglais, et un Maltais, qui trafiquent d'esclaves, et se rendent coupables des actions honteuses donc je vient de parler.'[8] Since Petherick was the only British subject in the Sudan, apart from Maltese, the allegation was immensely damning. At Petherick's instigation, Natterer wrote another letter dated March 1862 vindicating the Welshman by explaining that his report was incorrectly translated:

> I beg to inform you that in the translation of that report into French an unpleasant error has crept in. After I had described the bartering trade with the Negro populations as having suffered in consequence of the slave trade, I said that the Germans were settled here in Khartoum, and that Frenchmen, Italians, one Englishman, and one Maltese carried on *trade* upon the White River. The translator has erroneously taken this to mean *slave trade*. At that time I did not at all know who was carrying on the slave trade on the White River, and therefore not the slightest imputation was intended to be cast upon you, which fact I hereby acknowledge.[9]

Natterer's solicited apology does not stand up to close examination. If the Austrian only meant to refer to legitimate trade and not *slave trading* then was he exonerating all Khartoum traders? What were the 'shameful actions' (*des actions honteuses*) of the traders if not slavery? Was the translator likely to have mistaken legitimate trade for slave trading in his translation? The Natterer apology was not the only one solicited by Petherick as to his good character. Testimonials were obtained from Theodor von Heuglin, 'court counselor' for the state of Wurtemburg; from G. Thibaut, representing the French Consulate; and from M. L. Hansal, who replaced Natterer as Austrian Vice-Consul. Neither Heuglin nor Hansal knew about Petherick's commercial activities prior to 1859, while Thibaut, it was said, trafficked slaves as well as catching giraffes for the Regent's Park Zoo. Thibaut could have been protecting his own back when he wrote:

> I am astonished to learn that you have been accused of having carried on an illicit trade in Kordofan and on the White Nile. I can positively state that having for many years been your neighbour in Kordofan, I have seen nothing in your conduct that would warrant such a defamation of character. Like an honest man, you engaged in the regular trade of the produce of the country, such as gum and ivory.[10]

Every trader could produce someone to testify to his good character. Had not Petherick paid a warm tribute to his former partner, the infamous slave trader, de Malzac? On hearing of de Malzac's death, Petherick said:

> The most adventurous of these (explorers) ... my friend ... formerly an attaché at the French Embassy in Athens, who explored several of the tribes in the interior west of the Nile, in lat. 7° N, and whose recent death at Khartoum is much to be regretted, as I believe he contemplated publishing a work on the fauna of the White Nile, to which he was capable of doing justice.[11]

Petherick only ever admitted being involved in one *razzia* and that was accidental: a case of mistaken identity when his men seized six hundred cattle and fifty-three women and children from a village. The raid was intended to be in retaliation, but losing their way in the darkness his mercenaries attacked the wrong kraal. 'To avoid the ill-wind of my friend the chief ... I showed him the prisoners and informed him of the mistake,' said Petherick, adding:

> A short silence followed during which he seemed lost in reflection, then rising he spat in my face in a token of amity. Then in a long speech clothed in words of which many in the enjoyment of civilization and education might be proud he wound up [saying], 'You have repudiated the purchase of slaves, and have often told

me that your countrymen did all in their power to suppress slavery in every form, unlike ourselves who would consider your booty a rich prize. Give me then a further proof of your friendship by handing over the prisoners of my tribe, in order that I may rear living monuments to your generosity.' Jumping at the opportunity to 'rid himself of an embarrassment', the prisoners were released, the female captives so appreciative they refused to leave without spitting in his hand affectionately.[12]

Petherick ruled his mutinous band with an iron fist and the occasional thrashing. A big, fearless man, he refused to allow a recalcitrant rank and file to frustrate progress. Isolated from, and uninhibited by social constraints, he was uncomfortable in polite society, but in the wilderness a match for anyone, leading his renegades fearlessly and resolutely through a wilderness either roasted by the sun or beaten by torrential downpours into a sea of clinging mud.

If not a slaver on his own account, Petherick did, however, participate in one of the most shameful trading activities of the 19th century, involving as it did a monumental elephant cull. Lured by the prospect of large profits, he risked the deprivations of travel in equatorial Africa, the danger of hostile tribes, and the fragile loyalty of his mercenaries. Had he perished, as did many Europeans who dared venture into this fever-ridden land it would have been up-country, alone and forgotten, in some filthy native village without priest or physician. Most survivors took their profits and never looked back but the Welshman saw the Sudan as a Promised Land with an inexhaustible supply of riches if the locals could be persuaded to cooperate. Never flinching from risk and physical challenge, the man had strong will and an iron constitution. Hardship was incidental, not even the dreaded Guinea worm attaching to his leg while wading through a foul swamp denting his determination. Burrowing into the flesh, the worm is only extracted with care and patience. If the head breaks off, the body disappears only to reappear in some other part of its host, weeks, even months later. When the head first protrudes, the worm is turned slowly on a stalk of straw like winding silk on a reel. If there is resistance, the stalk is gently laid aside on the leg for a few hours until it's safe to resume winding. The procedure can take days; the victim in considerable pain for much of the time.

Petherick was described in *Blackwood's Edinburgh Magazine* as having 'an open eye, a strong hand, a good digestion and happy temper'. But he was also the reckless adventurer subduing savages with a mixture of 'audacity and prudence ... a man not given to threaten when he does not mean to strike, nor to strike when he does not mean to conquer'. From the evidence of his journals, caution, prudence, and a heavy hand were all essential for a White Nile trader. But whether dealing with Shillooks or Dinkas (the most populous), the Nuer or Bongo, or the Bari nearer the equator, the Welshman was in the final analysis a 19th century conquistador exploiting native ignorance and vulnerability. Removed from the restraints of Victorian England, his passiveness regarding the slave trade might partially be explained by the only official guidance he received as British Vice-Consul: 'to protect British trade against local monopoly'. Only after the arrival in Central Africa of the new Mrs Katherine Petherick did he begin to understand the fears and uncertainties behind tribal hostility. Previously, skirmishes, even pitched battles were commonplace and Petherick was indeed fortunate not to have fallen to an African spear as did several of his business associates. Alexandre Vaudey, the Sardinian Vice-Consul in Khartoum always lived on the borders of crime using his official status purely as a tool for promoting commercial interests until dismissed. But before leaving the Sudan, Vaudey led one last slaving expedition up the White Nile to Gondokoro where he was killed on 5 April 1854 in a battle involving 4,000 natives of the Bari tribe. What led to the explosion of violence is not entirely clear, other than on arriving at Gondokoro a child was shot by one of Vaudey's men, their boats attacked, and in the ensuing battle he and most of his followers were killed. As it happened, Alphonse Brun-Rollet who replaced him as Sardinian Vice-Consul was no better, using his position like so many others as a cover for slave trafficking.[13]

Although Petherick's account of his travels was criticized as a bland, bowdlerized narrative, hip-deep in exploits but avoiding more sensitive issues, he was, nevertheless, an astute ethnologist and collector of native artefacts. The Djour, he noted, used profits from trading iron goods to arrange marriages, which meant that 'however deficient in charms a woman might be', spinsters were unknown among the tribe:

Total nudity is held in contempt by the Djour, although their covering is reduced to the smallest possible amount ... The women would be handsome were it not for a disfiguration of the under lip, in which circular pieces of wood are inserted, varying in size according to age from a sixpence to a florin. The young women are naked but the married women wear large clusters of green leaves in front and behind, which, attached by a belt to the waist reach to their ankles. Clean in their habits, they are particular in the daily renewal of their costume from the bush, the numerous evergreens

and creeping plants affording them abundant material for that
purpose. The ankles are encumbered with bright heavy iron rings,
fully one inch thick, these tinkling together as they dance produc-
ing a peculiarly fascinating sound.

At the centre of a Djour village the heads of enemies were displayed upon
a trophy tree above a set of tom-toms hollowed out of tree trunks and used
to warn of an approaching enemy as the tribes were constantly feuding.
On one visit the alarm sounded and, fearing an attack, Petherick seized
his rifle and followed the natives into the bush. Nearing the summit of a
steep hill, he was overrun by Djour warriors in full retreat, leaping like
greyhounds over fallen trees and crashing through the tall grass. On seeing
Petherick they stopped, shouting, 'The White chief ... the White chief', his
appearance encouraging them to turn and face the enemy:

> Bounding forward they were soon out of sight ... Marching at the
> top of our pace we followed as best we could ... and at the bot-
> tom of a beautiful glade we again came up with them drawn up
> in line in pairs ... not a sound indicating their presence. Joining
> them, and inquiring what had become of the enemy [they] pointed
> silently to the bush on the opposite side. Marching accordingly
> into the open with my force of four men, and although unwilling
> to shed blood, I resolved that we would act as skirmishers ... the
> enemy advancing out of the wood to form a long line two or three
> deep facing us. I did not like to fire upon them [and] in preference
> continued advancing thinking the [sight] of my firearms would be
> sufficient. I was right. A general flight took place, some three to
> four hundred Djour passing us in hot pursuit. On their return, a
> complete picture of savage life I could not have imagined ... a large
> host of naked Negroes grasping bows, arrows, lances and clubs,
> wild gesticulations and frightful yells proclaiming their victory, and
> displaying the reeking head of a victim.[14]

That night the naked Djour women danced around the trophy tree to the
beat of the tom-tom, hurling insults at the heads of their enemies. His
stock of beads exhausted, and flush with ivory, Petherick led his troops
back to the river, arriving in Khartoum in June 1856. As was always the
case before leaving a territory he was the first to explore, Petherick claimed
exclusive rights to its future exploitation by establishing a station with a
contingent of mercenaries to trade for ivory during his absence.

Figure 16. *Native families in the Sudan on their way to a circumcision lodge.*

If evasive about the slave trade, Petherick's journal is explicit about native customs, describing at length the circumcision of a chief's nine-year-old son, and the sexual mutilation of the child's three small Negress slaves, aged six to seven. On the day of the circumcision the son was paraded on horseback, accompanied by clapping of hands and singing, before the children were taken inside the mutilation hut, and their shouts of joy turned to screams of pain. 'The poor girls, held down by several women, were scarified in such a manner as to lose all traces of their sex ... Their recovery required forty days confinement on an *angerib*, whilst ligaments attaching the knees and big toes together precluded all except a trifling change of position,' he said.

For survival in equatorial Africa, it was paramount for Europeans to exercise self-control about sensible clothing, healthy food and clean water. Dealing with the erotic tension arising from encountering mostly naked bodies was an entirely different challenge. In this regard sources are veiled and oblique, accounts complicated by the puritanical conventions of Victorian travelogues in which sexual contact is only ever hinted at. Young, healthy males spending long periods away from legal or sentimental restraints must have been tempted but readers are left guessing about the clues tripping off the pages of memoirs.[15]

This is not to say there were no enduring relationships between Europeans and Black African women not restricted to sexual gratification.

Native wives were drawn mostly from the more attractive Galla women of Western Abyssinia, some having an important part to play in the daily lives of their Khartoum trader husbands. The doyen of the European community, the Frenchman Dr Alfred Peney, took a Galla woman as his concubine soon after his appointment as the Egyptian Government's chief medical officer for the Sudan in 1850 and five years later married her in the Catholic Church. After Peney died from exhaustion near Gondokoro in 1861 in the arms of the young Italian adventurer Adolfo Antognoli on an expedition to find the source of the Nile, Antognoli married his widow Mme Marie Peney. When Antognoli died from yellow fever in 1864 she married his business partner, a Ferrarese Jew, Flaminio Finzi Magrini and retired to Cairo.[16]

Another young trader, Eugène de Pruyssenaere de la Wostyne, a well-educated member of a noble Flemish family from Ypres, wrote to his parents reminding them that since he was nineteen and old enough to marry, and having become African in his way of life he could not ask a European bride to accompany him on his travels but he had been given a young slave girl. 'After two months experience,' he continued, 'I am convinced she will suit me better than any European wife. She speaks Arabic with a rare perfection so that we can talk agreeably to each other … True, her education leaves much to be desired but I am daily trying to teach her and before long I hope she will become a competent housewife. So, I have a girl who owes me everything, whom I have educated to my satisfaction, who does not impose on me any other influence but my own, and brings no relations to make my life a misery.'[17] Pruyssenaere married the Galla slave girl Amina Mariam at the Austrian Consulate in Khartoum in February 1864, the union later solemnized at the Catholic Mission. Within a year Pruyssenaere, too, had died from fever, his widow promptly marrying the Austrian Vice-Consul. Very few Europeans took their wives to the Sudan. Petherick would, but of the others only the Sardinian Vice-Consul Antoine Brun-Rollet, after several informal unions with native girls, asked his Marseillaise wife to join him. She agreed only to become yet another victim of the climate and conditions. While Petherick in his journal and letters offers no clues as to his own liaisons before the arrival of his wife, the disproportionate focus of the narrative on native nudity suggests he was by no means blind to the temptations.

On his fourth expedition in December 1856, no sooner had Petherick arrived at his *zariba* on the White Nile and settled down with his pipe of *latakia* (tobacco) in the shade of a tree when a group of 'unclad maidens' approached. 'I was not deceived in my expectations,' he wrote later:

Some half-grown, sable, and unclad maidens, ornamented with beads of a variety of colors, tastefully strung, and worn around their necks, waists, and ankles, seemed to wait for an invitation before approaching too near ... My pretty guests had no sooner concluded a rather hasty barter than they retired [and] a still larger party of matrons and their full-grown daughters – the former inspired by love of gain, the latter with a greater desire for ornament than dress, of which they exhibited the utmost possible independence – now made their appearance with larger quantities of provisions.[18]

Petherick's journal is peppered with accounts of naked natives dancing around camp fires but he always stops tantalizingly short of mentioning physical contact. Information about sexual liaisons is seldom direct, the clues scattered as in a detective story. Personal observations are guarded, sometimes humorous and appealing, others racist and chauvinistic. How Petherick handled his 'economy of pleasure' will never be known.

Richard Burton and John Hanning Speke were struggling overland from Zanzibar in 1858 towards Victoria Nyanza when Petherick, heading towards the equator on another hunting expedition, was confronted by a party of warriors brandishing lances. Reputedly cannibals, they regarded Petherick as another meal but declined to make a move without their chief, a grey-headed old man who on returning to the village urged his followers to stand aside. 'His first wish was to examine my rifle,' recalled Petherick. 'Removing the cap I handed it to him. The most inexplicable part seemed to be the muzzle, which, instead of being pointed had a hole in it. Placing his finger therein, he looked at me with the greatest astonishment and, to give him a practical explanation, pointing to a vulture hovering over us, I fired.'

Before the bird touched the ground, the crowd was prostrate, groveling in the dust, as though every one of them was shot. The chief held his head in his hands, his eyes fixed with fear. Petherick continued:

I thought he had lost his senses. After shaking him several times, I at length succeeded in attracting his attention to the fallen bird, quivering in its last agonies between two of his men. The first sign of returning animation he gave was to put his hand to his head and examine himself for a wound ... after a repeated call from the old man they [the crowd] ventured to rise and a general inspection of imaginary wounds commenced.[19]

Petherick's final expedition into the interior before returning to Britain to visit family and friends, and to purchase a large stock of weapons, started from Khartoum on 27 December 1857, and ended with his return four months later. His destination was the equator which he was convinced was reached after a twenty-five day march from a lake feeding the Bahr Al-Ghazal (possibly Lake Ambadi) at the rate of nineteen miles a day. The journey passed through mainly Niam-Niam territory, but despite their reputation for cannibalism Petherick never once found evidence of it. The main problem was the need for four interpreters to conduct communications through the different languages. Something was evidently lost in translation when it was explained the Niam-Niam were licking their lips at the sight of his white skin but that they really preferred dogs! The Niam-Niam had thousands of slaves employed in the fields, for hunting and for domestic work. It was a sign of poverty for Niam-Niam warriors to do anything other than fight, their arms consisting of spears, a curved sword, an iron boomerang, and large oblong shield made from reeds. The rains commenced in February, lasting until the end of October by which time Petherick was within ten days of a wide, deep river flowing west, probably a major tributary of the Congo but with his stock of beads almost exhausted he turned north after establishing another station garrisoned by mercenaries. A hundred native porters were needed to carry his ivory, and before leaving there was a parting gift from the chief: his daughter, to be Petherick's bride when he returned the following season.

En route to Khartoum the expedition stopped at Gaba-Shambyl, the station on the Bahr al-Ghazal Petherick shared with de Malzac to collect a young elephant, a juvenile rhinoceros, and six rare shoebills (Royal *Balaeniceps*) for the London Zoo, as well as some preserved animal heads, including several new species all destined for the British Museum. By July 1859 he was back in Cardiff staying with relatives – but minus the live specimens for the zoo, all of which perished when his barges were swamped crossing the Nile cataracts.

CHAPTER 6

The Promise

PETHERICK'S RETURN TO BRITAIN coincided with the lionisation of John Hanning Speke as the first European to reach Victoria Nyanza which he claimed was the source of the Nile. But Speke was also at the centre one of the most acrimonious public disputes of the Victorian era when Richard Burton, his leader on the Victoria Nyanza Expedition set out to discredit him before the geographical establishment. While their competing candidates for the Nile's source – Speke's Victoria Nyanza and Burton's Lake Tanganyika – were the focus of the quarrel, bad blood had existed between the two former Indian Army officers since participating in a disastrous expedition to Somalia a few years earlier. Speke had insinuated that Burton's poor leadership on that occasion by failing to post sentries was responsible for the death of another member of the expedition killed when Somalis attacked the camp at night. There was also an unresolved dispute over money, Speke refusing to pay a penny more towards the cost of the expedition during which he was wounded and briefly held captive. To make matters worse for Burton, an official reprimand was entered on his Indian Army record.

Speke's wealthy mother settled the debt but the row between her son and Burton was destined to boil over. Both were strong-willed and stubborn, neither man ever taking a backwards step. In spite of their differences, however, Speke had agreed to join Burton's expedition to the Central African lakes region sponsored by the Royal Geographical Society in June 1857. While Burton remained at Lake Tanganyika recovering from disease and fatigue, Speke headed north to discover the great inland 'sea' which he named Victoria Nyanza. In the early morning of 3 August 1858 on reaching the brow of a hill he called 'Somerset' after his West Country home, Speke recalled how

> the vast expanse of pale blue waters of the Nyanza burst suddenly upon my gaze ... I no longer felt any doubt that the lake at my feet

gave birth to that interesting river, the source of which has been the subject of so much speculation and the object of so many explorers … so broad you could not see across it, and so long that nobody knew its length.[1]

Speke measured the lake's elevation as 4,000 feet (it is 3,700 feet) and after estimating the bed of the White Nile at Gondokoro (4° 44" North) to be 2,000 feet, guessed correctly that Victoria Nyanza was separated from the Nile by a series of rapids. Despite having explored less than one tenth of the shoreline without finding the lake's outlet, Speke hurried back to Britain ahead of Burton to announce *his* discovery – his rush to publish seen as a blatant attempt to deny Burton a share of the credit. Speke had a triumphant return as the conqueror of the Nile. Burton, on the other hand, limped home a few months later, thirsting for revenge, his appearance that of a cadaver, brown yellow skin hanging like bags, eyes protruding, lips withdrawn; the legacy of numerous attacks of fever. Not that he was a stranger to travel in remote and challenging parts. Burton was an infinitely more experienced explorer than Speke. Complex and multi-faceted maybe, but a hugely talented anthropologist, author and linguist considered by many to be one of the most distinguished products of 'this blessed plot … this England'.

Tucked away at the back of Burton's account of their earlier expedition to Somalia was what proved to be a prophetic observation on Speke's disposition: 'Before we set out he openly disclosed that being tired of life, he had come to be killed in Africa.'[2] Speke would die – killed in a mysterious hunting accident not in Africa but Somerset – the dispute with Burton unresolved. Before that, he was engulfed in a fierce controversy with a rival determined to expose him as a charlatan, his credentials as explorer and geographer suspect. 'Too many questions were left unanswered,' Burton told the geographical establishment. Speke had jumped to the conclusion that what he had seen from Victoria Nyanza's southern shore was one great expanse of water when there might easily be a series of unconnected lakes. No one, insisted Burton, could claim Victoria Nyanza as the source of the Nile until it was circumnavigated and the exit found. David Livingstone at first agreed with Burton that Lake Tanganyika was the more likely candidate although after Speke's premature death the missionary/explorer revised his opinion. But of all the jibes flung by Speke's adversaries, one of the most wounding was that he had wasted valuable time sexually fraternizing with native women.

But did not Speke admit as much in his journal? His account of fraternizing with native women was far more explicit than anything Petherick dared to mention in his memoirs. Before leaving England, Speke appeared to shun female company, the only women with whom he had any relationship his mother and sisters. But in Africa he shed his inhibitions, describing in detail how he consorted with the grossly obese women in the Karagwe court of King Rumanika. Fat was beautiful to Rumanika who force-fed his pretty 16-year-old daughter until she was too heavy to walk. Wives were fattened like geese, sucking on milk pots, some of the women 'quite lovely' according to Speke but as round as balls. Besides giving the fat naked African women piggy-back rides he measured King Rumanika's sister-in-law as four feet four inches around the chest, thighs two feet seven inches, each bicep almost two feet, with curtains of fat hanging from every protuberance. In return for the intrusion, Speke showed her 'a bit of my naked legs and arms' – it is hard not to suppose he gave her a view of something extra! Later, two virgins were delivered to his hut and while Speke does not say if the gift was accepted, he describes Rumanika's court as a place of 'unbridled licentiousness' and admits to a 'bit of flirtation' with his daughter, and to discussing the likely colour of their progeny. 'The mothers of these savage people,' he wrote, 'have infinitely less affection than many savage beasts of my acquaintance … for a simple loin-cloth or two, human mothers eagerly exchanged their little offspring, delivering them into perpetual bondage to my Beluch soldiers.' At his next stop, the kraal of King Mutesa where Speke spent four and a half months hunting, flirting and drinking large quantities of native beer, he admits to having a sexual encounter with the dowager Queen Mother whom he described as fat, fair and forty-five. He lay her on the ground, and felt her. 'She likes it,' he wrote later in his *Journal*, the first draft of which his publisher thought 'slightly indecent' and likely to scandalize Victorian England. Given this, Burton and his allies in criticising Speke's geographical claims could hardly be accused of muck-raking.[3]

Because the twenty-five days Speke spent exploring Victoria Nyanza's southern shore in 1858 had not produced the incontrovertible proof required by the Royal Geographical Society to prove this was the source of the Nile, he was asked by the vice-president Sir Roderick Murchison to take another look. By chance, Petherick having returned to Wales in July 1859 called upon Murchison to advise the Society of his successful navigation of the Bahr al-Ghazal, while reminding the president of their previous encounter more than twenty years earlier in the Hartz Mountains. One imagines the impact the Welshman had on the armchair geographers, the Society in its early days more like a gentleman's club. Loud, large, and expansive, with thick wavy brown hair and a luxuriant beard a foot wide, Petherick was the epitome of the wild-eyed African adventurer tripping off the pages of the

Penny Press, a prototype for Rider Haggard. Murchison seized the opportunity to introduce Speke to someone whose knowledge of Central Africa
was considered priceless. At that point, it was still undecided whether the
second expedition to Victoria Nyanza would proceed up the White Nile as
far as Gondokoro and then overland, or inland from Zanzibar as previously
with Burton. Speke was impressed, describing Petherick as 'the greatest
of all explorers in those parts'. But the son of a Merthyr ironworks manager, reared amongst the smokestacks and furnaces of Penydarren would
live to regret the moment he agreed to help Speke whose patrician roots
were deeply embedded in the English ruling class. After marrying into one
of the richest merchant families in Britain, Speke's father, a captain in the
Dragoons, retired to manage their estate, Jordans, in Somerset. Despite a
flying start, the younger Speke neglected his studies, declaring that 'a sed-
entary life made him ill'. His education was adequate but undistinguished,
and interrupted by periods of truancy. The handsome, fresh-faced young
man was sometimes impulsive and emotional rather than rational but had
nevertheless distinguished himself in action during the Sikh and Punjab
Wars, afterwards resigning his commission to pursue his dream: the source
of the Nile.

At first, Speke suspected that Petherick had personal ambitions to discover the Nile's source which was not the case, the Welshman's primary
reason for his homecoming not to canvass support for an expedition but to
buy a very large quantity of weapons, sufficient it was said to start a war!
After visiting family in Wales he planned to return to Khartoum in October
or November that same year (1859). In the meantime, Petherick petitioned
the Foreign Office to raise his consular status to full Consul. The petition –
written in the third-party style commonly adopted for official memorandum
– reveals Petherick as essentially a manipulative White Nile trader eyeing
promotion as another tool in his workbox. After pointing to Khartoum's
rapidly increasing trade in ivory and gum, in Abyssinian coffee, and south
Sudanese cotton and gold, he stresses its importance as a transit point for
British goods: textiles from Manchester, earthenware and glass beads for sale
in the interior:

> Mr Petherick is the discoverer of India rubber in Africa and found
> it about the 8° N. latitude in countries bordering on the White Nile
> of which he has several hundreds of weight with him at the present
> moment for inspection and trial, and if, as he flatters himself it will
> prove a valuable article, large quantities thereof might be obtained
> and form an additional article of export to Europe.

Independent of British subjects trading to and resident at Khartoum there are numerous Levantines under British protection trading between that city and Cairo, as also between the former place via Souakim [Sawakin] and the Red Sea to Bombay which latter trade is on the increase owing to the establishment of the Medjidi Steam Boats [the Majidiyya Steam Navigation Company established at Suez in 1858] in the Red Sea for the purpose of direct communication with all the ports thereof from Suez to Aden.

As Khartoum is nearly 1,200 miles from Cairo and the present postal arrangements as conducted by the Egyptian Government between the above places will not permit of communication by letter in less than thirty-five days to sixty days, to receive a reply to his dispatch addressed H.M. Consul in Cairo, Mr Petherick will have to wait three to four months.

Thus it will be clearly perceived that any person enjoying British protection at Khartoum, can with impunity, for the time just stated, commit offences, run into debt or be capable of misdemeanour and defying at the same time his creditors, the local Egyptian authority and the British Vice-Consul until the latter can report to Cairo and be in receipt of instructions from H.M. Consul, it being well known that the British Vice-Consul has neither the power to imprison nor to proceed judicially unless expressly authorized by his Consul so that before the arrival of that authorisation the party committing any such offence as above stated will have ample time to be beyond the reach of his own or the Egyptian authorities.

Mr Petherick begs leave to remark that cases of assault with intent to commit murder, and debt have occurred, and the consequences of his incapacity as Vice-Consul to act energetically and promptly have led to unpleasant intercourses with the Egyptian authorities and have tended greatly to lower his official influence, both with the Egyptian authorities as also with the British population of the Sudan.[4]

At that time the only British subjects in Khartoum and the Sudan – apart from some Levantines under Crown protection – were the Maltese de Bono family clan, Petherick's bitter trading rivals. The Welshman failed to mention that the sole and immediate beneficiary of his increased diplomatic status was: John Petherick. Only once would he use his new judicial powers: to clap the de Bonos, uncle and nephew, in irons for slave-trading! This might have been justified but it was irrelevant because by then Petherick had too many enemies, not least the Austrian Government whose interests on the White Nile he misrepresented by describing their missionaries as agents in the Austrian colonization of Central Africa. For this he reaped the whirlwind![5]

Petherick's submission to the Foreign Office in support of his promotion was clumsy, and poorly written. It also hinted at a previous failed attempt when Britain's then Consul-General in Alexandria 'declined to support [his application] through feelings of delicacy'. Whatever that impediment, Petherick was nonetheless confident his new application would be 'cordially supported' especially in view of his contribution to African exploration. For 'the purposes of trade he had penetrated into the African interior further than any other person,' he told the Foreign Office, and was the first to discover and navigate a large lake in the interior of the Bahr al-Ghazal region at about latitude 9° north and longitude 27 to 30. Because Petherick only ever had a compass for navigation, he was never sure of his exact location. But assuming his rudimentary coordinates to be correct, the lake referred to was possibly Lake Ambadi, a large expanse of standing water, fluctuating in extent and depth according to the volume entering from the Jur River. Despite this uncertainty it is churlish to suggest, as some have, that the Welshman's discovery of the Bahr al-Ghazal and Lake Ambadi was 'pure pseudo-travel'.[6] Substantiation for his claim to have reached the equator is less easy. From Lake Ambadi Petherick explored its principal feeder river, the Jur, which although often blocked by floating vegetation was at other times navigable for more than 300 miles as far south as Wau at the centre of a vast Nilotic plain on the fringe of Dinka country. Exactly how far south he got is not clear. Petherick relied for directions on local tribes although he must have visited the region previously to establish his *zariba* at Lungo. Locating his chain of *zaribas* on a map is difficult because of the bewildering assortment of names used for identical places and landmarks. The people he describes as Niam-Niam are more likely to have been the Azande (meaning 'great eaters') inhabiting either side of the White Nile in South Sudan, and westwards across the border into what is now the Democratic Republic of the Congo. In the 18th and 19th centuries the Azande were frequently confused with the Niam-Niam. Mundo was an Azande village roughly sixty miles west of Gondokoro but still 200 miles north of the equator. The Royal Geographical Society did eventually receive independent verification that Petherick had, indeed, reached as far south as Latitude 4° North. Before he died from fever, the French explorer Dr Alfred Peney wrote to the Society saying that when travelling sixty miles west of Gondokoro he struck 'the penultimate stage of Petherick's former expedition'. That was taken to mean the Welshman travelled even further south than Latitude 4° North. Announcing this to the

Figure 17. *The Azande (meaning 'great eaters') were believed to be cannibals but Petherick found no evidence of this.*

Society, the then President Lord Ashburton added, 'If this be the case – and the identity of the names of the places and tribes and geographical features leave hardly room for doubt – an enormous rectification becomes necessary in the estimated extent and direction of Petherick's itinerary.'[7]

Petherick was appointed H.M. Consul to the Sudan by the Foreign Secretary Lord Russell with an annual salary of £100 although not without a last-minute hitch. On account of a misunderstanding his jurisdiction was initially restricted to Khartoum where he was expected to spend nine months of the year. Since that was incompatible with his business interests he told Lord John Russell:

> For the protection of British subjects or trade my presence and influence is equally as much required throughout the different provinces of the Sudan as it is in the town of Khartoum.
>
> I would therefore respectfully suggest to Your Lordship that my consulate instead of being a local one and confined to Khartoum might, as my functions as Vice-Consul have hitherto been employed, represent the District of Sudan so whilst in the Sudan and the interior of the country I may be considered to be within the limits of my consulate. The sum of £100 is however inadequate to meet the expenses necessary to enable me to keep up a consular establishment with every degree of efficiency or respectability as I cannot employ less than three persons.[8]

The three members of staff were an Arab secretary for his official correspondence (suggesting his Arabic was poor), a Janissary (a Turkish soldier)
for personal protection, and a local Sudanese to deputize during his long
absences. The man left in charge in Khartoum during Petherick's absence
in Britain was Khalil Al Shamy (alias Michael Lutfallah) who mananged
consular duties with active participation in slave raids. Lutfallah's brother
Habashi, also a slave trader, was Petherick's agent on the Sobat River!

The Foreign Office finally agreed to extend Petherick's consular district
to the whole of the Sudan increasing his salary to £150 a year on condition there would be no further charge on the Treasury. Emboldened by
this, he then asked Foreign Secretary Russell to use his influence with the
Egyptian Government to allow him to import a huge consignment of arms,
ostensibly 'to carry out the objects of my mission … and for the defence
of upwards of two hundred men located at seven establishments amongst
as many turbulent and warlike tribes in countries bordering on the White
Nile'. On reading Petherick's shopping list Russell suspected the arms were
either for resale or to wage a private war in Central Africa: 500 muskets,
80 elephant rifles, 20 fowling pieces and smaller rifles, two punt guns,
12 hundredweight of gunpowder, and three tons of lead. The Foreign
Secretary cut the order by two-thirds.[9]

In the meantime, Speke, anxious to make use of Petherick's knowledge of Central Africa, suggested travelling together up the White Nile to
Gondokoro and south to the point at which the river was believed to exit
Victoria Nyanza. For that reason, Speke persuaded Petherick to draw a
map of the region as he knew it, ostensibly for publication in *Blackwood's
Edinburgh Magazine*. 'It was far from my thoughts,' recalled Petherick, 'to
court notoriety either as a traveller, or as an author and one of the most
urgent of my acquaintances to induce me to overcome my prejudices with
respect to publishing was Captain Speke.' The map arrived too late for publication, according to Speke, but the pressure on Petherick to participate
in the second Nile expedition intensified, the Royal Geographical Society
inviting him to deliver a paper. Having not long returned from Africa, and
anxious to spend more time with his elderly father, the paper was read in
his absence by the Society's assistant-secretary Dr Norton Shaw. Petherick
was still in Cardiff when Speke wrote again encouraging publication of his
memoirs. 'You would be a world-wide benefactor,' he coaxed. 'The interest
… is much more intense than you suppose … the public want what is
now kept secret within yourself. The Royal Geographical Society has not the
means of spreading anything about whereas *Blackwood* has a larger circula-
tion than anyone else.' Persuaded that he was capable of writing a popular

best-seller, Petherick postponed his return to Khartoum and settled down to compose in rough-hewn English *Egypt, the Soudan and Central Africa*. An invitation followed to spend a weekend at Jordans, the Speke family estate in Somerset. Understandably, after such a long absence, Petherick was anxious for rehabilitation into Victorian society. The weekend went well for the impressionable Welshman who was an immediate hit with Speke's sisters, not because he was the intrepid African explorer but because he was a clumsy Welsh 'hippopotamus' unable to use the Common Prayer Book! Speke's sisters found it hard not to giggle at their house guest.[10]

The reaction of Katherine Walshe must have been very different. Katherine was a 33-year-old widow and mother of two teenage daughters Frances (16) and Madeline (14), whom she raised single-handed after her husband, a civil servant, died suddenly. Nothing is known about how she and Petherick first met but within months they were married at Brighton on 31 October 1860. According to the census return, the following year the couple had a temporary address at 4 Russell Square, Bloomsbury before leaving for Africa.

Katherine was born on the Isle of Man, not Malvern as stated on census returns. Her father, Captain Charles Edelmann of the Royal Scots Guards, was of German origin. A younger sister Mona was the wife of a wealthy Liverpool accountant, Peter McQuie. Katherine described herself as being of 'independent means' and moved frequently following the death of her first husband. There is some suggestion she was a governess when Petherick came along but not in straightened circumstances unlike a surprisingly large number of middle-class Victorian widows. The belief that most were well-provided for through investments and insurance benefits was not the case. On average, civil servants never earned sufficient to insure their lives for a worthwhile amount. Widows and children of the middle class were often thrown onto their relatives for support and in some instances the parish. By remarrying, they regained that sense of belonging important in Victorian society.[11]

While Petherick was romancing Katherine, he was also engaged in lengthy discussions with Speke about the best route to take to Victoria Nyanza. Both agreed that was from Gondokoro so long as they had sufficient men to force a passage through the hostile tribal regions between there and the lake. 'If you think as I do that Nyanza is, in all probability, the true source, our object evidently should be to bear at once directly on it from any point on the river which is most convenient for breaking off from,' wrote Speke to Petherick in December 1859. A few days later, and without a word of explanation, Speke abandoned the plan for a joint assault on Victoria

Nyanza. The Royal Geographical Society, he told Petherick on 22 December 1859, had agreed he should take the inland route from Zanzibar as previously. Could Petherick travel up the Nile to meet him at some pre-arranged point? 'What a jolly thing this would be to accomplish,' he said, adding: 'You could do your own ivory business at the same time that you work out geography.'[12]

A few days later Speke wrote to the Society implying Petherick had agreed, when in fact nothing would be until well after Speke had embarked for Africa with his new partner, Captain James Augustus Grant, another Indian Army officer.[13]

It is clear from a close reading of all the correspondence that Petherick never *volunteered* to have boats, men, and supplies waiting when Speke and Grant arrived at Gondokoro after exploring Victoria Nyanza. All he did was advise Murchison at the Royal Geographical Society that if the explorers took the inland route from Zanzibar it was essential support was waiting when they reached Gondokoro by which time their provisions and beads for trading would be exhausted. Speke would have great difficulty feeding his men, Petherick warned the Society. If they failed to arrive between December and February it was very likely they would find the river level at Gondokoro low, the place deserted and no boats available to carry them down the Nile.

For Petherick to have funded the relief expedition 'gratuitously', as Speke later suggested, would have involved a personal investment of about £100,000 (at 2005 prices), twice as much as it was costing the Royal Geographical Society to outfit Speke's expedition inland from Zanzibar. It would also have been a costly distraction for the Nile trader whose immediate priority on returning to Khartoum was to make arrangements for the ivory stockpiled in his absence to be collected from his trading outposts, and to re-provision and arm the garrisons. That Speke had taken the initiative is clear from the March 1859 record of the *Proceedings* of the Society which states that having been introduced to Petherick by Murchison, Speke proposed they combined their resources to proceed together from Gondokoro, dependent upon the Welshman receiving the same financial support as the Government promised him.

In the following January Murchison announced that the Foreign Office was contributing £2,000 towards the costs of the Speke/Grant expedition from Zanzibar. By the time they sailed for East Africa on 27 April 1860, no firm arrangements had been made for Petherick to meet the two explorers with supplies and boats when they reached Gondokoro. The Foreign Office would have to cover his expenses, he said. Single-handed he had not the means to undertake such a mission. Murchison agreed that Petherick could 'scarcely be expected to do it at his own expense'. When the Government refused financial assistance the Society launched a public subscription to equip the relief expedition. When it closed, only £1,000 was raised, half what was needed. The contract Petherick eventually agreed with the Society was that he would have two boats, supplies and men waiting at Gondokoro from November 1861 to June 1862. In the event that Speke and Grant failed to arrive between these dates a search party was to be sent in the direction of Victoria Nyanza. For how long the search continued was left to Petherick's discretion. However, it was abundantly clear he was not obliged to keep boats and supplies at Gondokoro beyond June 1862. As it happened, Speke and Grant reached Gondokoro on 13 February 1863 – seven months beyond the deadline! Nevertheless, a boat was still waiting with supplies, but where was Petherick? Angry and vindictive, Speke embarked upon a vendetta against Petherick even more intense than the quarrel with Burton.[14]

CHAPTER 7

The Journey

I T MIGHT AS WELL HAVE BEEN A HONEYMOON CRUISE but for the fact that the Pethericks were leaving Britain indefinitely, he as the first British Consul in the Sudan, and Katherine to assume the duties associated with his new status. The return to Khartoum, however, was about much more than providing support for the Speke Expedition which had left Britain nine months earlier. The Pethericks took with them everything necessary to make a permanent home in Central Africa, including two European servants: one – a seamstress they christened 'Little Dorrit' – would desert them in Cairo and the other, a young botanist named Foxcroft would die from fever. Furnishings for the Consulate in Khartoum were ordered from Silver of London, Katherine's piano came from Hutchinson's, Petherick's binoculars from Carey's in the Strand, while the Royal Gunmaker Holland and Holland presented Katherine with a pair of pistols she was advised to wear at all times outside Khartoum. After providing Speke and Grant with boats and supplies at Gondokoro on the White Nile, Petherick and Katherine planned to continue south to search for another great lake they heard existed near the equator: Albert Nyanza. With this in mind, and in addition to all the instruments the Royal Geographical Society provided for taking measurements, the Pethericks provisioned an expedition that was to last two years, shopping for supplies at Fortnum and Mason, and at Crosse and Blackwell from whom Katherine purchased a large preserved ham to serve to Speke and Grant when eventually they reached Gondokoro. Petherick would always insist the agreement with the Royal Geographical Society did not oblige him to be present personally to meet the two explorers, but his preparations – in particular the purchase of the ham – implied there was every intention to rendezvous with Speke and Grant. From Cairo, the Pethericks travelled south aboard the *Kathleen*, the fastest and most lavishly equipped dahabeeyah on the Nile, accompanied by three similar vessels, one loaded with provisions and several tons of coloured beads for trading with native tribes, the second to accommodate other members of the expedition, and the third as stabling for a pair of Arab stallions and grooms. Travelling in style was not unusual for Europeans in Central Africa. When Stanley set out to find David Livingstone, a thousand native porters were needed to transport his possessions while in the bush he ate dinner off a solid silver service, not forgetting the brandy, an essential travelling companion for all African explorers.

Following a tearful farewell from family and friends, the Pethericks sailed from Liverpool aboard the S. S. *Pactolus* for Alexandria on 17 April 1861, the ship's master kindly allowing the newly-weds the use of his 'comfortable cosy cabin on deck'. In her journal, Katherine captured every precious moment of the romantic voyage:

> April 20th –We are in the Bay of Biscay; the weather very rough, but being excellent sailors, we enjoy it, though the sea drenches us occasionally.

> April 21st –A gale last night: we rose to watch the grand effect. Morning dawned bright and beautiful; the high sea subsiding, were able to take solar observations.

> April 22nd –A glimpse this morning of the Portuguese coast; weather charming. A shoal of porpoises roll around the steamer, as if trying to race with her … Caught my first glimpse of Africa, that vast land where my home is to be. Of Spain, with its sunny mountains and cool glades, we had wondrous peeps.

> April 24th – We were the only passengers, excepting Little Dorrit, as we called her, who, with Foxcroft, were in our service – the first a clever seamstress, the latter to assist in forming insect, bird and fish collections … A little tired lark sought refuge on board; we put it in a cage but it soon died.

> April 27th – Again a lovely day; the awning, which during the storm was taken down, was put up again and beneath its shade we read and write.[1]

The Pethericks were greeted in Alexandria on 2 May by the British Consul-General Richard Colquhoun. Only a few months earlier Colquhoun had welcomed another adventurous couple. The big game hunter Samuel Baker and his teenage wife Florence were bound for the Blue Nile for a safari along the Ethiopian border with Egypt. Writing to Christopher Rigby, the British Consul in Zanzibar on 20 July 1861 with news of the intrepid visitors, Colquhoun said, 'Petherick takes with him a stout, buxom wife. He will be joined [in the Sudan] by a great friend of mine, whom you perhaps know, Samuel White Baker, the Ceylon sportsman. He too takes a charming little woman with him – I much fear both these ladies may lose health, perhaps life, in their rambles.' But there was much more to Katherine Petherick than might appear from Colquhoun's condescension. She was patient, charming and hospitable whereas Petherick was stiff and awkward – a counterbalance to her husband's excessive exuberance though nonetheless proving equal in courage and endurance for which she was universally admired.

But what possessed this sensible Victorian widow to leave her teenage daughters for Darkest Africa? Despite the age difference, there must have been shades of the *grand amour* for the relationship to survive what became an ill-conceived, vainglorious adventure. Was it Petherick's bravura, physically strong and daring, she the trophy wife: the Consul's lady, albeit in Khartoum, a filthy outpost on the edge of civilisation? For the wives of the 19th century foot-soldiers of the British Empire such calls were routine and accepted without complaint provided they had their creature comforts. But what woman – even two centuries later – would elect to spend her honeymoon in the disease-infested swamps of Central Africa? Incredibly, she never uttered a word of recrimination when it all went horribly wrong, her confidence in Petherick's strength and purpose unshakeable to the very last. If anyone was deserving of criticism it was Petherick for allowing Katherine to accompany him on such a dangerous mission. Having navigated the White Nile and explored the adjacent territories so often in the past, had he become indifferent to the risks?

The European community in Egypt gave Katherine an enthusiastic welcome. Britain's first Consul to the Sudan and his lady threw themselves into the inevitable round of dinners, dances and picnics before boarding the *Kathleen* in Cairo for the voyage to Khartoum. Few Europeans dared venture that far, the ruins at Thebes, Karnac, and Aswan the usual extent of their Egyptian adventure. The Pethericks followed the same well-beaten tourist trail as far as the First Cataract and the Isle of Philae, an opportunity for the proud Petherick to introduce his young wife to friends and associates while impressing her with his savvy. But the *Kathleen* could go no further than the First Cataract, the river too low for the sailing barge to cross safely. Some of her cargo was unloaded on to camels, leaving the Pethericks to travel overland as far as Korosko to await the arrival of the boats.

Katherine expected Korosko at the desert's edge to be a town of some significance with a minaret or two illuminating the skyline, but all she saw was a cluster of dreary mud huts with the occasional date palm. Determined to make the best of it, she was laying the table for dinner outside their tent when the Venetian explorer Giovanni Miani arrived en route to Cairo. Miani had abandoned the Nile after his barge grounded in the shallows, from which Petherick should have anticipated the danger ahead. The river was still rising at Korosko, but further south the blistering sun of the dry season had left the muddy flood plains around Khartoum deeply fissured. November, when the north wind blew, was the most favourable time to sail from Khartoum to Gondokoro, a voyage that in normal circumstances took about six weeks. But the Pethericks who never left Cairo until July 1861 seemed in no hurry to keep the appointment with Speke and Grant.

Miani, dressed in Turkish costume with a voluminous turban, impressed Katherine as a 'fine old man of prepossessing experience', unaware that behind his long, snowy white beard was an occasional slave trader. The Venetian was another obsessed with finding the source of the Nile and if initials found carved on a tamarind tree were Miani's then he had got closer to it than any previous European travelling up the White Nile from Khartoum. Some thought the initials were Petherick's until Speke's partner Grant appeared to solve the mystery to the satisfaction of some when he inspected the tree:

Three or four miles from the right bank of the Nile at 3° 34½ N. lat., and 32° E long. ... the Turks informed us that a European had two years previously accompanied from Gondokoro as far this point, and had returned to Egypt from hence because the rains were heavy, and he had not sufficient escort to push further south. They did not know his name but described him as having a long beard, and said we should find his name cut upon the tree ... I visited the tree on which the European had cut some letters, but they were so indistinct that I walked twice round it before I could distinguish them. They were grown over with a thorny creeper and bark, and had been merely scratched in the wood. They appeared like AIAA. The centre letters were I and A, and the outer ones either A without a stroke, or part of W ... I at once concluded that the traveller was not English, because his letters were not deeply cut into the tree as an Englishman would have done, and also because the letters were curiously formed ... Not until we reached Khartoum did we find out for certain who this traveller must have been. His name was MIANI, a native of Venice, who has protested against our Nile being a proper Nile, because we have placed his tree in a position of latitude and longitude (obtained by daily observations) different to what he made it without scientific instruments.[2]

Katherine's disappointment with Korosko was offset by the arrival from Aswan of the boat carrying their Arab stallions, Luxor and Arab, which were exercised each morning before the sun was up. Surrounded by steep-sided fierce mountains, Korosko was as hot as hell, the sight of the Nile in the distance small respite. Sleep was impossible unless the sides of the tent were up, Katherine agreeably surprised that none of the locals intruded, or gave them a second glance. Nor did the native children pester them for backsheesh. 'The girl-children,' she noted in her diary, 'wore the *rachet*, a fifteen inch fringe of thinly-cut thongs of leather tied around their loins; the boys were in nature's livery ... young imps revelling in the dust and similar pastimes'. Nothing could dent Katherine's enthusiasm for Africa, not even the poisonous snakes and scorpions dispatched with a pair of pincers constantly at her side.

At Korosko, while waiting for the arrival of other members of the expedition, the Pethericks after their morning ride amused themselves shooting wild fowl on the river in the afternoons from their India-rubber boat which they inflated for the first time.[3] 'The servants were utterly dismayed, and entreated us not to push off from the shore,' recalled Katherine. 'The banks by this time were crowded, and many divested themselves of their scanty clothing, prepared to rescue us, so positive were they a capsize must ensue ... For two hours we remained on the water, allowing the current to carry the boat with it, and then pulling our way back. We had a fishing line but made no use of it, as a swarm of small fish, the whitebait of the Nile, leaped into the boat. They had evidently been pursued by a monster of the deep and took an acrobatic jump to evade him. We counted sixty-three of these delicious-eating morsels. By now there was no need of a lamp – we dined by the light of the moon.'[4]

The two other members of the Petherick Expedition were Dr James Murie, a Scottish physician, and the young botanist Foxcroft both aboard the *Kathleen* which arrived at Korosko with the rest of their small fleet all decked out in Union Jacks. 'When they neared, we fired, and gave a jolly English "Hip, hip, hurrah!"' wrote Katherine. 'The first thing I revelled in was a bath on board.'[5]

The *Kathleen* was unloaded except for the piano and some pet animals which were to continue upriver with the boats when there was sufficient water to clear the rapids. Everything else would be taken overland by camel across 233 miles of the Nubian Desert to rejoin the fleet at Abu Hamed. The desert route was preferred because it avoided the long westwards loop in the Nile but had been closed on account of bandits until Petherick intervened with the Viceroy on behalf of the Khartoumers to have it reopened.

Rain rarely fell in the Nubian Desert. Other than the occasional well there was not a drop of water along the trail, not a hut, not a bundle of wood to light a fire, nothing but sand and rocky ridges separating the barren *wadis* dissecting the desert between the Red Sea to the Nile. The shortcut across the desert still took almost two months, the camels managing but a few miles each day over the rocky sandstone plateau.

Seventy-four camels were hired to carry the Pethericks' baggage and equipment along ravines strewn with bleached skeletons, in one a bleak reminder of what awaited the unprepared and unwary: the graves of four Europeans, one named Mary Walton (21) who perished attempting the crossing the previous year. After the hyenas had finished with the corpses, only a few scattered bones remained to mark their last resting place. But the Pethericks did stop to erect a more permanent memorial to another European who had perished. Mr G. Melly of Liverpool had died from fever near the desert village of Gagee in 1851 while accompanied on a botanical expedition by his wife, two sons and daughter. Melly was buried in a crude brick tomb on the top of a low hill in a Muslim cemetery and his family, on hearing about the Petherick Expedition asked them to make a detour to erect a marble tablet at the spot. 'I am reminded,' Katherine wrote after visiting the tomb, 'to assure all travellers in hot countries that weak tea *without* sugar or milk is most acceptable to the palate, and thirst is soon quenched by it.'

Some days into the crossing, horses were swapped for camels, Katherine hanging a rifle on her saddle, beneath a large coloured umbrella. Wearing yellow Turkish boots and billowing trousers, and white flannel jacket with large pockets, she sprang into the saddle from her husband's knee, and adjusting an enormous straw hat wrapped in muslin set off, the camel snapping at anyone within range and moaning piteously. Petherick was soon at her side, 'every inch the African adventurer' with his brigand's hat, knickerbockers suit, and leather riding boots. 'He had quite a show of firearms surrounding his saddle, and was thoroughly at home,' Katherine recalled.[6]

The fierce heat of the day meant an nearly start with just a handful of dates for breakfast. On entering a narrow, dark ravine about halfway across the desert, their camel drivers suddenly dismounted, blocking their path with a wild dance. The ravine, Chashm il Bab – 'Portal of the Desert' – marked the beginning of a parched plain where many had perished. The camel drivers refused to go further unless paid double. 'These Arabs tell you that if you wish to return you must pay double,' Katherine noted in her diary. 'Willingly this fee was given, and they went on their way rejoicing.'[7]

The only European encountered on the crossing was the ornithologist Marquis O. Antinori, a Venetian acquaintance of Petherick's bound for Cairo with a collection of exotic birds. 'We found him a delightful companion during his short sojourn,' said Katherine. 'Petherick's men [on the Bahr al-Ghazal] were most kind to him; he was short of beads and they supplied him with sufficient quantity to carry him on to Khartoum. He said that had it not been for those men he must have starved, as money was of no value to the natives.'[8]

On 15 September Katherine sighted her first slave caravan. Mostly children, they were dragged along by donkeys while their owners rode dromedaries. Nevertheless, Katherine's enthusiasm for Africa was undiminished. 'Never from my memory can be effaced the glory of the sky – watching the rising and setting of the stars – all becoming familiar to us, and we greeted them by name – until the mighty sun appeared when moon and stars waxed faint and dim before his presence. How soon its rays made glad all animated things! Butterflies flitted about, insects began to chirp, and the birds flew hither and tither.'[9]

At Abu Hamed, the idyll was shattered by a plague of biting, stinging mosquitoes infesting the banks of the Nile. Katherine's only escape was to rush into the river, watched closely by an Arab youth squatting under a tree. The youth on being told by her bodyguard to move away drew a knife from a shoulder holster. Hearing the commotion, Petherick sprang from his tent and collaring the youngster gave him a thorough thrashing.

A boat was waiting at Abu Hamed to carry them on to Khartoum – but not the *Kathleen*. Failing to clear the cataracts, she remained stranded at Korosko waiting for the river level to rise. The *Lady of the Nile* was a poor substitute, lacking all creature comforts. The wind dropped the moment she sailed, and the crew 'singing lustily to frighten off the crocodiles' jumped into the river to manhandle the barge up stream.[10]

The sun was a fiery ball setting in the west when the feluccas headed out to welcome the Pethericks home on 15 October 1861. The nearer they got to Khartoum, the more incessant the gunfire, the shore lined with people cheering, so many friends waiting to greet her husband that Katherine was lost in the crush. At the Consulate, twenty or more servants greeted their arrival with a thrilling *zachareet*. 'When my husband embraced me and bade me "welcome home" I was fairly overcome,' Katherine recalled, continuing:

> Bye-and-bye tears of thankfulness relieved me, and I was able thoroughly to appreciate the luxurious dinner provided … the host of servants bearing each a dish, the cover of finely-plaited straw stained in many colours attracting my attention. The joy in their faces, the blessings, the shaking of hands at every available moment, the continued firing, the blaze of light … the wild beating of drums, made us all strangely excited … the Doctor began a speech but never finished it – his heart was too full.

For Katherine, Khartoum was exhilarating, breathless.

The next morning as they sat opening their mail Petherick's head dropped. His father had died, and also a nephew killed in a riding accident. There was another surprise waiting at the Consulate: Petherick's intended bride, the young native girl given him by the Niam-Niam at his station at Mundo! The Welshman having failed to claim her, she married his agent, Aberachman. Katherine thought it all so charming:

> her figure slight and graceful, her eyes the most beautiful I ever beheld … innocent confiding eyes. She was a mere girl, yet the mother of two children … Her labour was protracted … it suggested that if she drank of her husband's blood all would be well. He instantly opened a vein in his arm, to which she applied her lips, and sucked greedily the life fluid. The child saw the light shortly after.

Katherine was given a 12-year-old slave girl from the same tribe to train as her seamstress in place of 'Little Dorrit' who had quit their employment in Cairo to marry an Arab.[11]

Whereas almost every European who spent any time in Khartoum considered it a pestilential hole, Katherine found the climate 'delicious' not suffering a single day's illness since leaving England. Her advice for surviving in the tropics was simple:

> Regular exercise, no abandonment to the noon hour's sleep indulged in by the residents here, moderate living, rising before the sun, going to bed some three hours after its setting, and a careful regard to the chills and heat of the country. Flannel, here-so-far my detestation is indispensable … Paddy's great coat … keeps both the cold and the heat out.[12]

The days flew by all too quickly. Each morning before breakfast they exercised their horses on the plain outside Khartoum escorted by two armed militiamen carrying Petherick's shotguns. The breakfast gong sounded promptly at nine o'clock and afterwards they strolled together in Katherine's English garden before Petherick left for his office. During the morning Katherine played the piano, accompanied by 'the birds singing joyously, even parrot Polly doing her best to add to the harmony'. Dinner was at three in the afternoon, sometimes with visitors but there were few Europeans in Khartoum and the Turks never called. 'After dinner,' recalled Katherine, 'it was a walk on the shady side of the garden where the palms and fig trees are so numerous, or beneath the shelter of the vine where the grapes were forming.'[13] But the quintessential world Petherick had painstakingly created for Katherine at the heart of Africa – servants, leisurely rides in the country, and the archetypal English garden – was about to be blown away.

In accordance with his agreement with the Royal Geographical Society, Petherick on 15 November 1861 dispatched two boats commanded by his most trusted agent Abil il Majid to Gondokoro with relief supplies for Speke and Grant. With the north wind at their backs, White Nile traders allowed five to six weeks to reach Gondokoro where they remained until the following February loading ivory and slaves delivered from *zaribas* in the interior. The Pethericks planned to follow immediately with another four barges loaded with sufficient supplies to support their own expedition, which they would embark upon immediately on completing the commitment to assist the explorers. But they never left Khartoum until March 1862 – five months later – by which time the wind had changed and the river was low. The cost of providing succour for Speke and Grant soon exhausted the £1,000 subscribed by the Royal Geographical Society, and recruiting crews and mercenaries for his own expedition was proving even more expensive and time-consuming for Petherick. As was customary, every man demanded five months' pay in advance, some promptly absconding with whatever they could steal, usually muskets. To make matters worse, the *Kathleen* remained stranded below the cataracts with essential equipment for measuring the flow of the Nile at various places and for making other calculations. Petherick dispatched men overland on fast dromedaries to collect what was needed. Meanwhile he waited to raise additional funds from ivory sales to Arab merchants then en route from the Red Sea. When the Pethericks eventually sailed they were accompanied by 120 armed men, 30 donkeys to carry provisions and beads, and three horses. Donkeys were essential because with a war raging in the interior between slave traders and native tribes, it would be impossible to recruit porters. 'No longer [can they] distinguish friend from foe,' remarked Katherine, adding, '… the slave trade is lucrative … and no one is prepared to undertake legitimate trade.'[14]

Katherine's eyes opened wider to the reality of life in Central Africa when the Roman Catholic Mission at Gondokoro closed after a dozen of the brothers died from fever. The Egyptian Government's French Medical Officer Dr Peney was another victim of the appalling climate. After a memorial mass for the doctor Katherine retreated to the Consulate wondering who might be next 'in our little band'.[15] But everything in the Consulate garden was thriving, the flowers grown from seed she brought from England, as well as peas, lettuce and turnips. Only the potatoes failed.

Before leaving Khartoum on 20 March 1862 the expedition was joined by an American, Dr Brownell, as its unpaid botanist. At Gondokoro, seven hundred miles south, Petherick's agent Abil il Majid had waited three months with boats and supplies for Speke and Grant to emerge from the interior. By July 1862, when there was still no sign of the explorers, Petherick's contract with the Royal Geographical Society to provide support expired. In fact, the explorers would not reach Gondokoro until February 1863, eight months after Petherick's commitment ended. But when the *Lady of the Nile* eventually sailed from Khartoum the Pethericks had no idea what lay ahead. On her deck was a four-pounder cannon purchased from the Roman Catholic Mission; the cabins were stuffed with rifles, muskets, and fowling pieces; and in the hold all sorts of preserves, a large quantity of grain, stores of every description, and clothing. Petherick also had a punt gun with which it was possible to bring down fifty wildfowl with a single shot. The towering lateen-sails, Union Jack fluttering from the yard-arm, filled; and with singing and shouts of farewell drifting across the water, and small boats weaving around the *Lady of the Nile*, Petherick's four-boat flotilla was off in cheerful anticipation. Katherine wrote:

> I need not describe how great was the enthusiasm [at our departure]. The crowds ran along the banks of the river as far as practicable, whilst all on board were either attending to the ropes and sails, or firing, or playing their crude musical instruments – the *tarabooka* principally – and singing in their own wild but heart-thrilling manner; whilst the women on shore, sweethearts, wives or mothers, following as long as they could, *zachareeting* joyously; others throwing dust over their heads, so bitterly did they feel the parting, holding their little ones on high from time to time to catch a glimpse of the *aboo* or father.[16]

CHAPTER 8

The Race

UNKNOWN TO THE PETHERICKS there was trouble following in their wake. As they headed upstream towards Gondokoro, the wealthy big game hunter Samuel Baker and his young mistress were not far behind. Petherick believed the Bakers were on safari on the Blue Nile; they had even agreed the couple could use the Consulate to rest before heading back to Cairo at the end of their trip.

Instead, Baker was about to turn the search for the source of the Nile into a race – a race he was unlikely to win given Speke's head start but one in which he counted on coming second by providing succour for the victors. A frustrated big game hunter seeking greater recognition than that bought with a bagful of trophies, Baker saw an opportunity to assume the mission entrusted by the Royal Geographical Society to Petherick. His excuse, that he was merely in the right place at the right time to assist Speke and Grant when the Pethericks went missing, feared murdered, fails close examination. By his own admission, Baker's sights were set firmly on carving a niche for himself in African exploration long before setting foot on the continent.

Arriving in Khartoum from his Blue Nile safari, Baker's boats were loaded with additional supplies 'in the hope of meeting Speke and Grant'.[1] And when rumours circulated that the Pethericks were dead, Baker seized upon their misfortune to offer assistance to the missing explorers, persisting in this even when he knew the rumours were untrue.

Baker envied Speke his public acclaim after discovering Victoria Nyanza on his expedition with Burton to the Central Lakes region. There was much the pair had in common: a shared love for distant places and enthusiasm for hunting. Both were from the same part of the West Country, their families acquainted. Both found it hard to settle, Baker describing himself as 'unhappy when unemployed and too proud to serve'.[2]

An opportunity to emulate Speke first arose when Dr David Livingstone was recruiting for a Government-backed expedition to explore the Zambesi River. Excitedly, Baker asked a friend, Lord Wharncliffe, to intercede on his behalf with the Foreign Secretary Lord Clarendon to find him a place on the Livingstone expedition. 'I should amazingly like to form one of the party,' he told Wharncliffe. Clarendon passed the letter to Sir Roderick Murchison at the Royal Geographical Society who consulted Livingstone. Baker's application, Livingstone decided, was 'out of the question' because he had nothing useful to contribute. Disappointed but not defeated, Baker offered to fund a second expedition along a different route, at which point the Foreign Office intervened advising the Society that Baker's presence might jeopardise Livingstone's expedition by alienating the Portuguese in Mozambique.[3] Thwarted, Baker found another interest: shooting wild boar in Eastern Europe in the company of a rich Arab, this culminating in his purchase of the teenage Florence in a Transylvanian slave market. Reluctant to return to English society with his young slave mistress, Baker was casting around for another challenge as Speke finalized plans for his second expedition to Victoria Nyanza. But he was too late – Grant was already chosen to accompany Speke with Petherick providing support. The nearest Baker got to the expedition at that stage was a chance meeting with Petherick at a soirée for explorers and hunters arranged by the retired admiral Henry Murray at his rooms in Piccadilly. As it happened, Murray was the brother of Sir Charles Murray, the British Consul-General in Egypt on whose recommendation Petherick was appointed honorary Vice-Consul in the Sudan ten years earlier.

Baker was travelling again in Eastern Europe with Florence when he wrote to Petherick from Constantinople, reminding him of their meeting at Admiral Murray's rooms and asking for help. He planned, he said, to spend two or three years hunting elephants in the Sudan. Could Petherick provide a letter of introduction to help him outfit an expedition? 'If you could give me a letter to anyone in Khartoum who could put me up to the right men and the right plan for a first go at the elephants, I should be exceedingly obliged,' he wrote. Baker mentioned only elephants, nothing about his interest in the source of the Nile.

Whether or not deliberately duplicitous, there is no doubt Baker had designs on the Nile before arriving in Africa and admits as much in his memoirs:

> I had not the presumption to publish my intention, as the sources of the Nile had hitherto defied all explorers, but I had inwardly determined to accomplish this difficult task or to die in the attempt. From

Figure 18. (above) Sir Samuel Baker, hunter/explorer, who provided support for Speke and Grant when the Pethericks were reported murdered.

Figure 19. (right) Lady Florence Baker (née Florenz Sass), the teenager who became Sir Samuel's mistress, then wife after he rescued her from a Transylvanian slave market.

my youth I had been inured to hardships and endurance in wild
sports in tropical climates, and when I gazed upon the map of Africa
I had a wild hope, mingled with humility, that, even as the insignif-
icant worm bores through the hardest oak, I might by perseverance
reach the heart of Africa.

I could not conceive that anything in this world had power to
resist a determined will, so long as health and life remained. The failure of every former attempt to reach the Nile source did not astonish
me, as the expeditions had consisted of parties, which, when difficulties occur, generally end in difference of opinion and retreat.[4]

Was Baker expecting, perhaps hoping, Speke and Grant would fail to prove
that Victoria Nyanza was the source of the Nile, leaving the way open for
his solo attempt on the legendary river? As a wealthy man of leisure, he had
the time and means necessary to pursue his goal without restriction. But
there was one problem: Florence. 'Had I been alone it would have been no
hard lot to die upon the un-trodden path before me, but there was one who,
although my greatest comfort, was also my greatest care … I shuddered at
the prospect for her should she be left alone in savage lands at my death,'
wrote Baker. But Florence resolved 'to share all dangers and to follow me
through each rough footstep of the wild life before me'.[5]

Remarkably, Florence – Lady Baker after Samuel was knighted for
naming his single most important discovery Albert Nyanza in memory of
Queen Victoria's Prince Consort – and Katherine Petherick were not the only
European women heading for Gondokoro in 1862. A courageous but ulti-
mately foolhardy Dutch heiress, 24-year-old Alexine Tinné, hired a steam
boat – the first seen on the White Nile – to transport herself and mother
Harriet, her aunt, Madame Adriana la Baronne van Capellan, and two Dutch
maidservants to Gondokoro. From there, the group intended travelling
overland to Victoria Nyanza and the source of the Nile. Baker was astonished when told, writing to his brother, 'They are bent on discovering the
source of the Nile. They must be demented. The young lady is now by herself with the Dinka tribe and the mother goes up by steamer tomorrow. They
really must be mad … all the natives are as naked as the day they were born.'
The arrival of the steamboat was a sensation in Gondokoro but mother and
daughter were forced to turn back after Alexine fell ill. Harriet noted in her
diary that the best way to keep well was 'to avoid draughts, wear flannel
around the loins, and an "English" diet of fruit and well-cooked vegetables.'
Such was the interest in the source of the Nile that Baker suggested that
some enterprising individual should open a public house on the Equator![6]

The intervention by the Bakers would not have been a problem but for Petherick's disastrous decision to abandon the river for the more circuitous overland route. By sticking to the river, even though late in the season, he could have reached Gondokoro before the Bakers left Khartoum. The river journey had, however, started badly, the *Lady of the Nile* rammed and holed not long after leaving Khartoum. No sooner was she baled out, and the barge following with doctors Murie and Brownell lost a mast in a sudden gust of wind and grounded. The boat with the donkeys also came to grief, a sail rent by the wind and one of the crew injured. With all repairs complete, they were once again weaving past wooded islands, Katherine plucking blossoms 'like yellow butterflies' from the overhanging mimosa trees. At Gaba Shambyl they learned that the entire region was disturbed; hundreds of Shillooks enslaved; and the river filled with boats, holds packed with slaves.[7] Where once natives gathered to trade ivory, the banks were deserted, villages burned or abandoned. In one creek, seven slave boats flying the Turkish flag were moored. In response, Petherick hoisted the Union Jack and fired the two-pounder on the deck. 'There are hundreds of slaves – men, women, and children – beneath the trees,' he told Katherine, 'and thousands of cattle around. It is a horrible sight! They are Dinkas, I think. There are Baggaras with their horses, hired to hunt them down.' That night, nine slave boats passed them on the river, and at dawn thousands of cattle were being driven along the bank. 'Early in the morning another slave boat floated past,' wrote Katherine, 'one poor, old white-haired Negro seated in the bow, his face covered by his hands, which were clasped above his knees, his attitude eloquent of grief and despair. The slaves were chiefly women and children huddled together. In some part of the deck straw matting, suspended on poles, afforded them protection from the sun.'[8]

The wind dropped, the temperature at noon was 110° F in the shade, the crew jumping into the river to tow the barge while four mercenaries stood guard. Kaka, one of the largest of the Shillook villages with six hundred *tookuls* (straw huts), was abandoned. More and more slave boats swept pass, others loaded with stolen grain, their crews singing merrily. The captain of one told Petherick there had been a huge *razzia* led by Baggara Arabs. Five hundred slaves were seized as well as twelve thousand cattle. Now they were heading downriver to divide the spoils.[9] Not long afterwards, eight natives were seen lying on the riverbank, all shot to death.

Passing the mouth of the Sobat River their small fleet was struck by a violent storm, torrential rain flooding the cabin. Katherine sat amongst the wreckage surrounded by people and pets, and a gazelle on a sofa. The day was damp, cold and cloudy, she wrote, adding:

Petherick went out early to shoot. It is of the utmost importance we should be careful with our preserved provisions, as we all understand this will be a protracted journey. By noon Petherick had not returned. I was becoming uneasy but he had met a tribe prepared to barter ivory for beads, [and had] fearlessly approached his nude and new-made friends armed with lances, their bodies covered with wood ash, hair stained red. The pipe of peace was smoked and three tusks were bartered for beads, lance and hatchet-heads.[10]

On 5 April a boat approached from Gondokoro raising hopes the *reis* (captain) might have news of Speke and Grant. All he knew was that Petherick's agent Abd il Majid had left for the interior in search of the missing explorers as instructed. At sunset Petherick's crew were still towing the *Lady of the Nile* through the still water, praying for a breeze to relieve their toil. When the wind died, it rained, the downpours ruining everything on board, wrote Katherine:

April 17: A breeze at sunrise! Vast quantities of floating plants were carried downstream; they looked so compact that it appeared as if a green field had launched itself into the river. An hour brought us to the entrance of the Bahr al-Ghazal which was then free of weeds and the stream was running with force. The river now took an abrupt winding to the south-east; the banks could only be seen from the mast, as the reeds were of great height and advanced far into the river. The breeze having failed, the round-robin towing was resumed.

April 29: Colds and coughs. One in particular who having little faith in the ordinary treatment, gave himself into the barber's hands, who, with a razor was about to cut off his tonsils which, he said, were of no use in the man's throat. This was prevented by Petherick. On another occasion, one of the crew accidentally bruised his instep. He appeared one day with his foot bleeding profusely. Inquiring the cause, he replied that he had cut it out with a razor in three places, as that was the best way to cure the bruise. His foot is now in a sad state and he is unable to use it.

Another sprite of a man – 'Blondin' we call him – made a complaint that one of his shoulders had slipped lower down than the other, and unless the Consul could pull it up again he could not work. Petherick called for a hammer and a long nail, and placing the man in proper position, prepared to raise the arm. A light dawning suddenly on 'Blondin' that the nail was about to be employed in fastening his arm in its place, he declared he was better, and we soon saw him with the towing line in hand.

May 8: At daybreak a cry was heard that the *Lady of the Nile* was filling. The *reis* on diving discovered three leakages. All of us baled and the cargo was flung on shore. Many packages were ruined; and the sun would not shine forth to brighten our difficulties. Saw for the first time the lotus plant.

May 9: It is Petherick's birthday, and we cannot be joyous – all things tend to depress us. The *reis* expresses doubts as to our onward progress; wind and current are against it.

A few days later and without knowing it, Katherine met the 19-year-old Maltese slave trader Amabile de Bono. The Pethericks were asleep when their *reis* hailed two boats approaching from Gondokoro to ask for news of Speke and Grant. 'When the sun was up,' wrote Katherine, 'a young trader "A" came on board but had heard nothing of the travellers. His ivory station was beyond the cataracts of Gondokoro some six days journey from that place. He described the country as very beautiful and healthy. He remained on board a short time ... then continued his journey to Khartoum.' Amabile de Bono was the most youthful European trader on the Nile, and the only one with the initial 'A' and a *zariba* beyond Gondokoro at Falaro in which Petherick had a financial interest. For some reason, Katherine decided not to identify their mysterious visitor in her journal.

Katherine's knowledge of slavery in the Sudan came mostly from her own observations. Her husband might have expressed disgust but not once during his tenure as British Vice-Consul had he taken steps to suppress it. Katherine's arrival coinciding as it did with his promotion to Consul, together with new Foreign Office guidance to deal firmly with slave trafficking, left Petherick in a quandary when three boats flying the Union flag approached the *Lady of the Nile* on 19 May 1862. 'We felt sure the travellers, Captains Speke and Grant, were on board,' Katherine noted. 'Up went the flags, and Petherick, forgetting his precept to the men never to waste powder, commenced the firing, those on board the approaching boats returning the salute, [and] though still some distance off, they were recognized as ours.' The anticipation that finally they were about to meet the missing British explorers was palpable. Cases of wine were opened and other luxuries prepared for Speke and Grant. While Katherine decorated the cabins, Petherick formed the crew on deck, *tarabookas* beating a welcome as the boats drew closer. The Pethericks had letters for Speke and Grant from family and friends, and there were toasts to drink to the victors. Training his binoculars on the first boat Petherick recognized it as one of those dispatched to Gondokoro six months earlier with supplies for Speke and Grant.

The midday heat was unbearable, the wait equally so as the *Lady of the Nile* fired a salute, and everyone on board waited patiently for Speke and Grant to appear on deck. Moments later Petherick exploded angrily. The explorers were not on board: only Abd il Majid, the Arab agent entrusted to deliver boats and supplies, and mount a rescue mission if Speke and Grant failed to arrive at Gondokoro. This was to prove a pivotal moment for John Petherick, ruining his reputation and casting a cloud over the remainder of his life. The account of what followed is pieced together from Katherine's diary, Petherick's official dispatch to Colquhoun, the British Consul-General, and the sworn testimonies of crew members.[11]

While Petherick was interrogating Majid about the missing explorers, Katherine blurted, 'This man has brought down slaves and they are in his boat.'

'Impossible! Are you sure?' asked Petherick. She was. A servant, Katherine, sent to search the boat's hold had found seventeen slaves.

'Be patient until I've finished,' said Petherick leading Majid down into the hold. According to Katherine, Majid appeared 'unconcerned', more interested in showing Petherick the two cheetahs he had captured:

> I could hear Petherick's assent, *'Badaen'* (bye-and-bye) ... He then went below – oh, what a time it seemed to me that he remained there! At last he came up, Majid with him. I saw from his face pale with anger that he had made a discovery, but calmly he said to the reis [of the slave boat], 'Take down your flag' (our dear English Union Jack) ... Petherick seizing it and rolling it into a ball flung it on board the *Lady of the Nile*, crying passionately, 'Never more shall it be disgraced by floating o'er this boat again.'

Majid was clapped in irons and thrown in the hold, and the slaves tethered below released into the blinding sunlight. 'With outstretched arms I received them,' wrote Katherine. 'Young girls and little children – I had only tears.' On returning to the *Lady of the Nile* Petherick brushed passed Katherine, muttering, 'Do not speak to me just yet – this is a bitter and great trial. I must be alone.' Was this Victorian over-dramatization, or a contrived reaction to impress a wife who, for the first time, faced the possibility her husband might be involved in the slave trade?

And there was worse! Boats belonging to Amabile de Bono whom Katherine met only a few days earlier had passed the *Lady of the Nile* under cover of darkness. Told that de Bono was also carrying slaves, Petherick gave chase downriver in a felucca but after boarding de Bono's boat and detaining him for two hours failed to find any slaves. More than a hundred, however, were discovered by Dr Murie packed into the holds of a second boat owned by the Maltese who was detained and clapped in irons alongside Majid. The night was not over. Another barge in the convoy commanded by Aga Khurshid – de Bono's agent at Falaro – had dozens of slaves shackled together with *shebas* in appalling conditions. On a fourth boat owned by a Frenchman, Barthélemy, Dr Murie found yet more slaves crammed beneath the hatches.

At a stroke – and possibly against his better judgement – Petherick, by arresting Majid and Amabile de Bono, and shipping them back to Cairo for trial, antagonized most traders on the White Nile. No one had before broken the unwritten code that protected the Khartoumers' illicit traffic. If Petherick did have a hand in it, then blowing the whistle was almost certain to provoke a backlash of the very worst kind – that during his years in the Sudan the Welshman also dealt in slaves either on his own account or indirectly.

Indeed, Majid's defence was that he was only following orders; that he made no attempt to evade Petherick on the river, and that Petherick knew of his approach three days *before* their boats met. As for Speke and Grant, Majid had, after delivering the boats and provisions to Gondokoro in December 1861, travelled to the station at Wayo five days' march from Gondokoro to organise the search for the missing explorers. Too ill to lead it himself, another man, Mussad, led a search party to within fifty miles of a large lake, possibly Albert Nyanza before being compelled to turn back by a terrible famine raging across the country. There was no sign of Speke and Grant.

Outraged over the use of his vessels for transporting slaves, Petherick wrote immediately to the British Consul-General in Alexandria urging the detention of de Bono the moment he was delivered to Cairo, where his uncle Andrea de Bono was also being investigated for trafficking. Petherick wrote:

> I need hardly mention how necessary it is to be severe with the Maltese Amabile not only on account of his guilt but to strike terror into the other Europeans in this country who to my knowledge are carrying on the same disgusting traffic. In one word, legal commerce from Khartoum to Gondokoro is at an end … trading with the natives is out of the question … they are prepared for fight or flight … when the opportunity offers attacking and murdering crews.

> Fearful and sickening circumstances have occurred under my own eyes in my voyage thus far and trustworthy reports of similar acts further up the river are daily turning up.[12]

The younger de Bono, Petherick alleged, was responsible for organizing many of the *razzias* up-country, causing the terrified tribes to flee deep into the interior the moment Europeans approached. But the Nile traders turned the tables on Petherick by making him the focus for a whirlwind of recrimination. Instead of Petherick demonstrating by the arrest of Majid, de Bono, Aga Kurshid, and Barthélemy that his hands were clean, almost every Khartoum trader signed a statement accusing the Welshman of being a slave trader. In Cairo, Amabile hired a good lawyer to petition the Consular Court to the effect that Petherick had trumped up the slave trading charges to protect his own interests on the White Nile. 'Did he actually see them [the slaves] himself or was it reported to him?' Amabile asked the Consul-General, continuing:

> I brought down a large quantity of goods with me. This appears to have excited his jealousy and given rise to this accusation against me, he being a merchant as well as a consul. In the latter capacity he exercises his authority over British subjects on the slightest pretext who may be in the same line of business as himself so far as to compel them to quit the neighbourhood ... this to secure himself all the profit.[13]

Before the case came to court de Bono's lawyer submitted depositions sworn before the Governor in Khartoum alleging that Petherick had ill-treated slaves on the White Nile and was directly involved in the slave trade. The Welshman was not, said de Bono's lawyer, 'the upright character generally expected of one of Her Majesty's functionaries ... not a trustworthy man'.[14] The charges against de Bono and the others were dropped for lack of evidence, leaving Petherick having to defend himself against their allegations. In the opinion of Sir Edmund Hornby, Judge of the Supreme Consular Court, delivered on 8 August 1862, the Crown's case against both de Bonos, uncle and nephew was untenable. The conduct of the nephew was undoubtedly suspicious, he said, but Petherick had failed to gather reliable evidence. The most the judge could do was warn Amabile and all other British subjects trading on the White Nile of the dire consequences if found to be directly or indirectly implicated in the slave trade. Petherick was reprimanded for a botched investigation, for being disposed to present hearsay as evidence.

More seriously, the judge concluded that it was probable that the British on the White Nile were no better than any others, a thinly disguised reprimand for Petherick who was the only British trader on the river. But there was little the British Government could do about this so long as the Egyptian and Turkish Governments tolerated slavery, added Sir Edmund.[15] To make matters worse, Majid, caught in the act of trafficking was only briefly detained by the Egyptian Governor at Khartoum while the Frenchman Barthélemy also walked free. Petherick had no opportunity to defend himself against the charges because at the time he and Katherine were struggling to survive in the bush – might even be dead, according to some reports.

In her version of events Katherine suggests there was stronger evidence against the four men the Consular Court judge had not heard. According to an entry in her diary, Majid, after waiting for Mussad's return from the failed search for Speke and Grant, proceeded to Gondokoro to join the huge *razzia* led by Baggara Arabs. The raid netted 351 Black Africans and three thousand head of cattle which were divided according to each trader's contribution. By the time Majid encountered Petherick on the river, most of the slaves were sold.[16]

The conspiracy against Petherick gathered momentum while the consequences of attempting the journey up the White Nile too late in the season mounted. Upstream the rains had started, and the river was flooding thousands of square miles as it flowed south. The *Lady of the Nile* was holed a dozen times, clothes and provisions soaked in muddy, evil-smelling water. The American Dr Brownell died from fever, his few salvageable belongings auctioned amongst the crew. Progress was painfully slow, and with little wind the boats were towed through endless reed beds.

'Our people are losing heart,' wrote Katherine:

> The towing is very dreary work: the small boat carries our line to the reeds in advance, and we are pulled up by it, taking the line to our consort [second boat] so that when we are stationary she in turn pulls up to us; then off goes the felucca again with our line, and so on. The canoe is worked in the same way to assist the doctor's *dahabiya* ... the *Lady of the Nile* is nearly done for ... another serious leak.

On 17 June they sighted a cluster of huts surrounded by a thick fence of brambles, but already an island in the flooded bush. Further on they were met by canoes from the Poncet brothers' station at Lolnum and advised to wait at the Gaba Shambyl station until the rainy season ended.

The *Lady of the Nile* sprung yet another leak and ran aground crossing a small lagoon. Petherick decided it was impossible to travel further by river. Recalling that moment, Katherine wrote, 'Petherick did not rave as he was wont to at the negligence of the *reis* [captain] and crew … He was completely overcome: a man's silent grief is hard to witness.' But he refused to turn back to try again the following season even after canoes ferrying provisions ashore from the stricken *Lady of the Nile* were attacked by natives. They would continue overland, southwards to his station at Wayo, a village in the Neambara and only a few days' march west of Gondokoro. The Neambara was a huge area extending from the Congo to the Nile. To reach it and the station at Wayo, the Pethericks would have to traverse the Aliab Valley, a low-lying flood basin running parallel to the Bahr al-Jabal (the Mountain Nile). In the rainy season the valley was transformed into a vast swamp, dotted with lakes, some several miles wide and ringed by belts of papyrus. For good reason the Poncet brothers who hunted elephants in the Aliab advised against attempting the overland route. It was now July and the worst possible time of the year, every small depression flooded and infested with crocodiles. Why then, when Petherick was only 150 miles by river from Gondokoro did he choose the impossible? Barring disasters, it was certain to add weeks to the journey, even in the dry season. In fact, it took another seven gruelling, treacherous months.

What remained of the rigging on three of the boats was transferred to the fourth so that at least one might succeed in getting through to Gondokoro with supplies for the missing explorers. Petherick knew from questioning Majid that the boats he had sent earlier were no longer on station at Gondokoro; that they were most probably being used to traffic slaves. Although his contract with the Royal Geographical Society terminated in July 1862, he was honour-bound to keep his verbal promise to Speke not to leave him stranded in Central Africa. By July Gondokoro would be deserted and without supplies and transport down the river the explorers might easily starve or be killed by natives. The only reason Petherick could have had for not taking the only serviceable boat on to Gondokoro was that the overland detour led through lucrative elephant country. The three crippled boats were to return as best they could to Khartoum where the *Kathleen* should be waiting if she had finally cleared the cataracts and, following repairs make a fresh attempt to reach Gondokoro in November when the wind was more favourable. Despite his vast experience of the interior, Petherick failed to anticipate the risks travel lingoverland would mean for his wife and the entire expedition.

With a small Union Jack fluttering from the point of a lance they entered the swamp on 1 August 1862, splashing through a narrow channel between walls of tall reeds, the water soon above the fetlocks of the horses. After crossing a lagoon in the India-rubber boat, the horses swimming at their side, the march was resumed. Katherine was dressed for the journey: a short thick linsey petticoat, leather gaiters, strong boots, cloth jacket, leather gloves and straw hat. Around her waist she buckled the five-barrelled revolvers given her by Holland and Holland of Bond Street.[17]

That night, shadows flitted to and fro, the flames from the camp fires lighting up ghostly visitors plastered in white ashes. Petherick thought an attack imminent. Fitting new firing caps to Katherine's revolvers, he whispered, 'Be prepared! The Negroes are rising.'[18] If the attack came Katherine was to stand at the centre of the ring of defenders. But instead of hostile savages springing from the darkness, it was a lion, which made off after seizing one of the native women for supper.

A week later a skirmish did occur when negotiations to purchase native canoes to cross a lake broke down. The first wave was driven off, Petherick setting up a defensive position in the centre of a field of native corn. There they would remain, he told the attackers, eating their grain until the rainy season ended and the lake could be forded. The natives, having been assured by a shaman that rain rendered their enemies' weapons harmless, attacked with showers of poisoned arrows and spears until Petherick dropped their leader from 300 yards. 'The man was no sooner down,' Petherick recalled, 'and one of mine in true Niam-Niam fashion administered the *coup to grace* to the head.' At the height of the battle, Katherine was confronted by a naked native with matted hanging locks, lance and shield. Raising her revolver to fire, she suddenly recognized one of their Arab soldiers who always fought masquerading as a native.[19]

Although agreeing eventually to supply canoes for the lake crossing, it was a ruse for the tribe to launch one last attack. An advance party sent ahead with the baggage to find a suitable landing place on the opposite shore was ambushed, canoes overturned, the men clubbed and speared as they struggled in the water. Had not Katherine been suffering from a severe bout of fever, she might have been among the casualties, the incident the probable source of the rumour that they had been murdered or drowned. After the ambush she begged Petherick to take her out of 'this unwholesome spot'. Lifting his wife in his arms, the Welshman waded through the swamp to the India-rubber punt moored at the water's edge waiting to be towed across the lake by a native paddling a canoe. Fearing more treachery, Petherick cocked his gun and gave Katherine a knife to cut the tow rope if the native made a false move. The sun was directly overhead, the tall reeds their only shade, the punt moving slowly through the still water towards the only visible patch of dry ground – a large anthill. From its summit Petherick surveyed the flooded landscape stretching as far as the horizon. By now Katherine was desperately sick from wading through mile after mile of filthy, evil-smelling water. Fearing the worst Petherick noted in his journal on 20 October 1862:

> My poor wife suffered seriously from rheumatic and gastric fevers. Dr Murie told me to prepare for the worst, and I had received, as I feared, her last words. He and I were watching her last night when she suddenly asked for food. Murie who throughout her illness had been unfailing in his attentions, proceeded to get something or other. We had been without tea, sugar, or any of the many comforts so necessary for an invalid – wine, brandy, all had been lost in the lagoon. Soon the doctor returned with some boiled grain in a paste, sweetened with honey, into which he had put a little *araki*, distilled on the premises from grain. This the poor patient with difficulty swallowed, and she knew us again. For days, water only had she taken – not food of any kind. The doctor shaking my hand said, 'The crisis has passed; she will recover.'[20]

Katherine struggled on bravely, always at her husband's side, never once complaining as they trekked through a region no Europeans had crossed, and where the natives thought strangers fell from the sky. As their provisions dwindled, they slaughtered most of the donkeys. When the horses died, nothing was wasted – not even the rats caught at night in the Pethericks' tent. In the dry season the Aliab Valley was flush with game; in the wet there were mostly crocodiles.

The lake ambush had cost the expedition dearly. Of what was salvaged, arguably the most important were the baskets of coloured beads, essential for hiring porters from the tribes in the Aliab Valley. But on reaching the valley the beads were worthless, cattle now the only currency. Without native porters they would almost certainly perish. Reluctantly, Petherick permitted his Arab mercenaries to raid native villages for cattle:

> My men's demands for cattle to purchase their different requirements rendered them troublesome and turbulent. They told me we could neither return nor proceed and they would consent no longer to privations, whilst possessing of the means [weapons] to obtain them [cattle], and with or without my consent they were prepared to join

in a *razzia*. I gave my reluctant consent ... in lieu of cutlery or cloth as articles of barter ... When glass beads begin to lose their charm the traders disgraced themselves by descending to the level of the savages ... in their attempts to enrich themselves by the plunder and destruction of tribe after tribe. From this [comes] slave-stealing, which, according to my experience, all the traders more or less indulge in. With the produce they pay their men, and realize such profits that many believe the ivory trade is but of secondary importance.[21]

Only dire necessity had persuaded him to permit the *razzia*. If any slaves were taken the culprits would be delivered to the authorities in Khartoum for trial, he warned.[22] A month later his mercenaries returned with hundreds of cattle – and dozens of slaves: evidence, according to Petherick's critics, of his involvement in the slave trade.

Christmas 1862 was miserable. The Pethericks were both ill and only able to travel a mile or so a day, nowhere near the seven Petherick usually covered in these parts. The rainy season was ending but as the floods subsided so did the freshwater streams disappear. Drinking water was scarce, every evening a new well dug. But the elephants were back and Petherick was hunting and buying ivory from the Azandes whose territory they entered on New Year's Day 1863. The Azande reputedly ate their dead, it being customary for the intestines, heart and lungs to be removed and given to the women of the tribe to make into a stew. The mutilated corpse was then rolled in a mat and, suspended three feet from the floor of the hut, smoked until mummified, remaining in that position amongst the grieving relatives for twelve months, after which it was buried.[23]

The country was tinder-dry and fire an ever-present danger as the expedition wound its way single file through a sea of tall grass. Suddenly, a column of smoke spiralling into the sky signalled the approach of a bushfire racing like an express train, flames leaping towards them, the hot blasts threatening to suffocate the men trapped amongst the grass. Fortuitously, they stumbled upon an open space cleared by the natives as a refuge:

Rapidly our people came to the same haven, all safe; a few of the cattle only had been lost in the fire. The little plot of ground was too small for the assembled party, so forming a circle we stamped and beat down the burning bush for some distance around ... in less than an hour we resumed the march over still-smouldering herbage, causing many of the unshod to utter cries of pain.

At the River Ayi the expedition rested beside the first running water seen for several weeks. Resisting the temptation to spend longer on a riverbank flush with vegetation, they pushed on. Petherick was riding one of the few surviving donkeys at the head of the column when suddenly there was a shout and he rolled in the saddle. Katherine was at his side within seconds, breaking her husband's fall as he collapsed to the ground. 'He's dead,' someone cried as Dr Murie emptied a skin of water over Petherick's head. But he was only unconscious and by the next day, the fever having subsided, Petherick was well enough to lead the expedition into his *zariba* at Wayo.[24]

CHAPTER 9

The Succour Dodge

WEARING A RAGGED CALICO DRESS bought from an Arab after her clothes were lost in the Nile, Katherine Petherick at last reached her husband's station at Wayo. Hair crisp like brittle straw, face seared red-brown and too painful to touch, Katherine's only protection from the sun's fierce rays was a grubby turban. At least the painful blisters had healed leaving her hands like crimped brown leather. As worn and haggard as any native, the terrible ordeal was far from over, the 33-year-old now aged beyond recognition by the dreadful journey across disease-ridden swamps, through flooded forests, and plains burnt tinder dry by a pitiless sun. A journey that should have taken no more than six weeks aboard the *Lady of the Nile* became a nightmare lasting ten months.[1]

A group of native dancers welcomed the weary travellers to Wayo. All were slaves taken in a *razzia*, but most having found husbands among Petherick's garrison at the station had no desire to return to their villages. While resting, the Pethericks were astonished to receive a letter from Samuel Baker waiting at Gondokoro with boats and supplies for Speke and Grant. In fairness, Baker was not alone in believing the couple had perished. The news of their death had reached Khartoum from missionaries acting upon notoriously inaccurate 'native reports' of the sinking of the Pethericks' canoes after they were ambushed. The unsubstantiated account found its way to England and into *Field* magazine, the author of the article demanding vengeance if it was true that the brave explorer and his courageous wife were murdered by natives:

It is our duty as Englishmen not to sit quietly down and accept for the truth the news of his having been drowned but to call the murderers, or those who have power over them, to strict account; and this is not only because Petherick was the fine brave fellow we all knew him to be, but because he was the emissary of the British Government, as Consul at Khartoum, as well as commander of an expedition to render assistance to Captains Grant and Speke in their arduous, dangerous, but important explorations.[2]

Not unnaturally, the Royal Geographical Society cast around for other means to assist Speke and Grant believing that Petherick's last known position, if still alive, was 'in the Neambara' 300 miles west of Gondokoro. The confusion arose because 'the Neambara' was commonly used by Nile traders to describe a vast area extending from the headwaters of the Congo to the Nile. Unable to locate Petherick's station at Wayo on any map, the Society assumed he was lost in the Neambara and asked Baker, already en route to Gondokoro, to provide assistance for Speke and Grant. In fact, Wayo, which Petherick reached in February 1863, was only sixty miles from Gondokoro – but Baker had already seized his chance to earn a place in history.

Petherick would become both a casualty of Baker's ambitions, and victim of Speke's slanderous accusations. But did Baker warn Speke of the allegations swirling around the Welshman in order to win his confidence, or had Baker real evidence of Petherick's involvement in the slave trade? After reading Baker's letter Katherine had no doubt there was a conspiracy afoot. Her husband was too charitable by far, she thought. 'There are serious intrigues against you in Khartoum,' Baker wrote to Petherick. 'Upon your arrest of Amabile [de Bono], an accusation was sent to the Consul-General, including the official declarations of two Consulates, charging you with some former participation in the slave trade. Of course, the seals of numerous natives ornamented the document.'[3]

Katherine had absolute faith in her husband's integrity and honest desire to suppress the slave trade. Baker's actions were malicious, she decided. Had he not known before leaving Khartoum that they were alive and that Speke and Grant, already many months overdue, had still to reach Gondokoro? Communication between the two places was reasonably good between October and February, the river busy with traffic, besides which the *Lady of the Nile* had limped back to Khartoum with news that the Pethericks were alive and heading overland to meet the missing explorers. Furthermore, the *Kathleen*, the fastest boat on the river, after being provisioned had sailed immediately for Gondokoro. Baker should have known his intervention was not needed.

As it happened, the Pethericks, Speke and Grant reached Gondokoro within days of each other in February 1863 – the explorers almost a year overdue, the Welshman and his wife by their own reckoning ten months late. Baker's dream of being the first to the source of the Nile was snatched away; his only hope to provide succour for the victors.

If the decision to travel overland accounted for Petherick's delay, then the four and a half months Speke spent at the palace of King Mutesa was largely responsible for his late arrival. Speke's explanation was that Mutesa was reluctant to allow him to leave. After all, Speke was the first white man he had ever seen. For his part, Speke revelled in the intimate attention he received from the women at the court, and declared himself pleased with his 'natural history specimens' – two twelve-year-old girls. He finally dragged himself away on 7 July 1862, and two weeks later sighted the White Nile exiting Victoria Nyanza – 'a magnificent stream from 600–700 yards wide, dotted with islets and rocks, flowing between high grassy banks'. Speke followed the river until it plunged over the Ripon Falls, which he named after Lord Ripon, president of the Royal Geographical Society at the time of his departure from England. The falls were only forty miles east of the king's palace where he spent so long socializing. The discovery, however, still failed to silence critics. Speke's mistake was in not following the course of the river exiting Victoria Nyanza far enough to prove, convincingly, that it eventually became the Nile.

On 3 December he and Grant marched into the station at Falaro to bursts of celebratory musket fire, and a drum and fife band – and hugs from Muhammad Wad el-Mek, the Sudanese commander of the mercenaries at the *zariba* belonging to Amabile de Bono and Petherick. For the final leg of their journey to Gondokoro the explorers were accompanied by six hundred porters and slaves carrying ivory. The nearest *zariba* to the equator, Falaro had for three years been at the centre of a bloody war with the Bari whose villages were plundered and burned, men, women, and children rounded up like cattle and sold. Petherick's reputation was not helped by his business interest in Falaro, which he on at least one occasion described as 'my station'. In fact, when Speke reached Falaro and asked Wad el-Mek who was his 'master', the Sudanese replied that it was 'Petrik' [sic] then on his way to Falaro. So why was Wad el-Mek not flying the British flag, asked Speke. To which he replied they were 'de Bono's' colours. Not having heard of de Bono, the explorer asked again, 'Who is de Bono?' to which Wad el-Mek replied, 'the same as Petrik [sic]'. According to Robert Brown in *Africa and its Explorers* (1893), Amabile de Bono before his detention for slave trading had instructed Wad el-Mek to render assistance to 'Petrick's friend' – apparent confirmation that the Welshman did have an interest in Falaro and, rather than neglect his obligations to the explorers, went to some length to provide help.[4]

By now, however, every trader on the Nile knew that Petherick had blown the whistle on the slave trade. Kurshid Aga, the Circassian indicted by Petherick after slaves were found aboard his boat, was already back in business at Gondokoro having successfully pleaded that whatever he was accused of was outside Egyptian jurisdiction. In the circumstances, it would have been surprising if Muhammad Wad el-Mek had not taken the opportunity to malign the man responsible for exposing the slave traders.

Petherick's interest in Falaro was not the only piece of circumstantial evidence his enemies could draw upon to drag him down. The de Malzac connection was another. Admittedly, in mid-19th century Sudan the opportunity for social intercourse was infrequent and not to be missed. In a territory with so few Europeans and where no questions were asked, discriminating between associates was rarely an option. Most had something to hide, not least the Frenchman de Malzac who died from syphilis in 1860 screaming obscenities at the priest administering the last rites. In mourning the passing of a 'friend' Petherick could have been referring to an earlier partnership in the ivory trade before the Frenchman blazed a path into slave trafficking for others to follow. Driven insane by syphilis, de Malzac had been taken forcibly to Khartoum by his own mercenaries to face a charge of murder upriver. Among the small group of mourners at his graveside were two young slave girls, one with a child aged four de Malzac had fathered, the other pregnant. Another mourner was Josef Natterer, Austrian vice-consul in Khartoum.[5]

Within a few days of leaving the station at Wayo, and after crossing a range of low hills, the Pethericks saw in the distance a pair of rust-coloured sugar loaf peaks rising over 3,000 feet behind Gondokoro. As they neared the river, Katherine became euphoric about the slightly undulating countryside dotted with 'graceful tamarinds with their health-sustaining fruit … the country captivating … huts detached … with well-kept gardens'. Then, spotting the *Kathleen* moored among the slave boats on the White Nile she burst into tears of relief.[6]

The arrival of the Pethericks in Gondokoro only five days after Speke and Grant hardly warranted the angry outburst with which Speke greeted the Welshman and the shameful way he treated Katherine. Baker might have poisoned his mind and Speke, after an exhausting expedition, was perhaps not entirely in control. But the manner in which he turned on Petherick was reminiscent of the controversy with Burton following the first journey to the Central African lakes, and in sharp contrast to his last letter to Petherick. Dated 28 March 1862, it was a friendly invitation for

Petherick to join the fun at Mutesa's palace. How it got to Petherick is not explained, but one assumes it was by native runner:

> This is to invite you up to Uganda for the King is very anxious to meet you. I dare say this may somewhat interfere with your trade, and so create some pecuniary loss; but depend upon it whatever that loss may amount to I will ask the Government to defray it, for it is of the utmost importance that the country should be open to trade, and no opportunity could be better than the present. You will have to drop your dignity for the present, and to look upon me as your superior officer; on asking Mutesa what presents I should write for, he said, 'Don't say anything about it lest he should think that I Mutesa coveted his property more than himself.' So to quiet him, I said he did not understand the matter – that I ordered you to come up the Nile to look for me and bring me away and that three vessels were mine as well as their contents, and you should not disobey my orders. I do not know what things you have but bring a lot of pretty things such as cheap jewellery, toys, pretty cloths, glass and china ware; one or two dogs of any sort for the King's emblem is a dog; and any quantity of powder and lead for he shoots cows every day ... bring fez caps for my men to wear as a guard of honour ... your men may be armed up to the teeth. I have lots of beads for the way back to the boats. Grant is at Karagwé with a game leg and I am sending boats for him. His last letter to me is enclosed, also a map of the country which you had better send to England, together with this, by your first opportunity. I would go across the Massai country at once to Zanzibar but considering you promise to keep two or three boats two or three years for me, I sacrifice everything to fulfil the engagement. A photographic machine would be useful here for the court is very splendid.[7]

Speke regarded the discovery of the river plunging over the Ripon Falls as mission accomplished – conclusive proof that he was right about Victoria Nyanza being the source of the Nile. The egotism that bared its face in the quarrel with Burton now turned on Petherick. The explorer was not about to share any part of his triumph, certainly not with a tough Nile trader with a reputation for slave trading!

To make matters worse, the first person Speke and Grant met in Gondokoro was Kurshid Aga camped with hundreds of traders and mercenaries along the White Nile loading their human freight aboard barges for the journey downriver. At Gondokoro they were beyond the law, and when not drinking, quarrelling, or abusing their prisoners, they fired off their muskets indiscriminately, bullets humming through the air in all directions day and night. If the fiery furnaces of the Welshman's home town were often described as the 'ante-room to hell' then Gondokoro was hell itself and Petherick a marked man. In a letter to the *Times* published on 23 July 1863, Baker said:

> Not a day passes without natives coming to me with tales of their wives and children being carried off, their cattle stolen, the defenders murdered. The traders' establishments here are full of slaves, women in fetters. The whole of the traders who now infest Gondokoro and the neighboring country are Egyptian subjects with the exception of Andrea de Bono.

Baker plainly meant Petherick when he added, ominously, 'No trader – and I make no exception – can carry on his trade without stealing cattle and murdering the owners.' In Baker's opinion, by deliberately exciting unrest among the tribes, the traders had made Central Africa impossible for legitimate trade. 'Gondokoro is a perfect hell,' he noted in his memoirs, adding:

> It is utterly ignored by the Egyptian authorities, although well known to be a colony of cut-throats. Nothing would be easier than to send a few officers and two hundred men from Khartoum to form a military government, and thus impede the slave trade; but a bribe from the traders to the authorities is sufficient to ensure uninterrupted asylum for any amount of villainy. The camps were full of slaves, and the Bari natives assured me that there were large depots of slaves in the interior belonging to the traders that would be marched to Gondokoro for shipment to the Sudan ... I was a great stumbling block to the trade, and my presence at Gondokoro was considered an unwarrantable intrusion upon a locality sacred to slavery and iniquity.[8]

After the interminable marshes, Gondokoro provided firm anchorage above the flood plain, the riverbank sloping gently upwards to the red-brick ruins of the Austrian Catholic Mission, abandoned without a single convert, the missionaries mostly dead. Below the ruins a cluster of mud huts beneath two shady sycamores marked Gondokoro on the map for only two months of the year. Afterwards it was deserted, the traders heading downstream with their human cargoes, the mercenaries left behind to launch further *razzias* on the unfortunate tribes so that when the boats returned the following November more slaves would be waiting to be shipped.

On entering Gondokoro and asking Kurshid Aga about Petherick's whereabouts, Speke recalled, 'A mysterious silence ensued; we were informed that Mr de Bono was the man we had to thank for the assistance we had received ... and then, in hot haste, after warm exchanges of greeting with de Bono's agent, we took leave, to hunt for Petherick.'

But instead of Petherick they found Baker. 'Guns firing in the distance; de Bono's ivory traders arriving, for whom I have waited,' Baker noted in his journal at the time. 'My men rushed madly to my boat with the report that two white men were with them who had come from the SEA! Could they be Speke and Grant? Off I ran and soon met them in reality. Hurrah for old England! They had come from the Victoria Nyanza from which the Nile springs. The mystery of ages solved. With my pleasure of meeting them is the one disappointment, that I had not met them further on the road in my search for them ... When I first met them they were walking along the bank of the river towards me ... At a distance of about one hundred yards I recognized my old friend Speke, and with a heart beating with joy I took off my cap and gave a welcome hurrah! I was totally unexpected; my sudden appearance in the centre of Africa appeared to him incredible as I ran towards him.'

At first Speke failed to recognize the bearded stranger until reminded of their last meeting ten years previously aboard a P&O steamer at Aden, homeward-bound from India. 'What joy this was I can hardly tell,' wrote Speke. 'We could not talk fast enough, so overwhelmed were we both to meet again.' In a report of their meeting to the Royal Geographical Society, Speke said Baker 'was hoping he [Speke] got into difficulties so that Baker might help him out.' In February 1863 after the Pethericks were reported missing (but no longer feared dead) Baker misinformed the Society that they were heading away from Gondokoro to trade and that for this reason he was sailing immediately for Gondokoro.[9]

Anxious to leave for Khartoum as soon as possible to telegraph Murchison that 'the Nile was done,' Speke accepted Baker's offer of boats and supplies even though Petherick's *Kathleen*, the fastest on the river, was waiting.[10] When the Pethericks marched in four days later, they found that the explorers were using the *Kathleen* but only temporarily – and had taken a bottle of brandy from its stores to celebrate the discovery of the Nile flowing out of Victoria Nyanza.

A misunderstanding is the only charitable explanation for Speke's hostility. Having sailed for Africa before the agreement between Petherick and the Royal Geographical Society was finalised, he was perhaps expecting too much. The society never asked Petherick to wait at Gondokoro beyond the June 1962 deadline; nor was it necessary for him to be there in person as Speke might have supposed from their last conversation when the Welshman promised to do everything possible to provide support.[11] The search party might well have found the explorers had Speke taken the anticipated route from Victoria Nyanza – instead of wasting time fraternizing with tribal chiefs and their women.

In the case of Grant, he was very much the bystander, apparently content for Speke whom he admired immensely to receive all the acclaim. At first, the Pethericks were grateful for his impartiality, even friendship. But after Speke's tragic death, Grant indebted to the memory of his leader also turned against Petherick, accusing him of negligence and the misuse of public funds. In his account of the confrontation in Gondokoro, Grant noted in his memoir *A Walk Across Africa*:

> But where was Petherick? Had he made no preparations for us? Or, finding, we were not able to keep time, had he despaired and given up the search? A handsome *diabeah* and luggage boat of his were here, but there were neither letters nor instructions for us. He himself was not at Gondokoro and had never been there. Instead of cooperating with our own expedition he had gone to his own ivory depot in the west, and only arrived at Gondokoro four days after ourselves. We learned from Baker that kind friends in England had placed £1,000 in the hands of Mr Petherick for our succour, and were doubly surprised he had made no effort to meet us. It was to M. de Bono's men, and not Mr Petherick's that we were indebted for our escort. I feel it due to the memory of my companion to state these facts, and to say that I had the same feeling of disappointment he had, and that our meeting with Mr Petherick was by no means the cordial one we anticipated.[12]

'A woman clothed in unwomanly rags,' was the reflection Katherine Petherick saw in the mirror aboard the *Kathleen*. Her native servants were horrified, kissing her hands and murmuring *miskeen* (poor thing). No one expected to see the Pethericks alive. It was evident that Speke and Grant had made themselves comfortable aboard the *Kathleen*, their luggage, writing and drawing materials scattered everywhere, as if they had 'just left for a stroll'. According to Katherine the blame game started immediately Speke and Grant returned to the *Kathleen* to gather their possessions. Instead of a cordial reception, Petherick was met by coolness and rejection. Sipping tea with the explorers Katherine tasted only the bitterness threatening her husband. She tried to warn him that Baker intended seizing the kudos, but 'Petherick so honest and true himself believes everyone the same, and would not listen to my fears that Speke and Baker wished us not well'.[13]

They were surrounded by enemies. The occasional musket round ricocheting off the deck of the *Kathleen* was a reminder the slave traders had Petherick in their sights. But the deterioration in his relationship with the slaving community was more profound than his bungled attempt to prosecute the de Bonos. Pragmatism might have dictated his reaction to the slave traffic during the previous ten years, but the situation had changed by the time he returned to Khartoum from England as Consul in 1861. In his absence, he claimed, slave trading became rampant, implying it was not previously a problem. The Foreign Office was unconvinced.

The Pethericks attempted to heal the wounds between themselves and the explorers by inviting them and the Bakers to dinner aboard the *Kathleen* shortly before Speke and Grant were due to depart for Khartoum. The occasion must count as one of the most memorable in the history of exploration, in the same league as Stanley's meeting with Livingstone. The night was as usual hot and humid, a million mosquitoes beating their way to the dinner table, their tiny corpses smeared across the cabin window. The cabin was oppressive; the atmosphere charged with hostility. In the distance guns popped. The clank of iron and screams of pain echoed through the darkness where, out of sight of the snooping Europeans, fetters were being fitted to the latest arrivals from the interior. The wooden yokes locking heads and shoulders in a vice on the long march from the *zaribas* were removed and iron rings attached to their ankles welded in place by blows from a large stone.

The evening aboard the *Kathleen* was remarkable: uniquely so, if only because so many British subjects were gathered together in so remote and desolate a place beneath a full moon on the White Nile – closer to the heart of Africa than any compatriot had ever been. Baker was already claiming that *he* was the first Englishman to reach Gondokoro as Katherine served the large preserved ham from Crosse and Blackwell that had survived the Pethericks' hungry march through the wilderness. At first the conversation was polite but edgy. Soon it veered towards open warfare, Petherick for his part insisting he had fulfilled his mission, and Speke, supported by Baker, disagreeing vehemently. The Welshman said Speke had no right to expect more than two boats and men waiting with supplies at Gondokoro, whereas there were four, at least one of these on station from November 1861 to June 1862. Petherick's boats and supplies had, in fact, remained there eight months longer than the deadline agreed with the Royal Geographical Society, apart from a few weeks when they were used illicitly by his agent Majid to transport slaves down river. Since all parties involved were many months overdue, the controversy seems in retrospect to be entirely irrelevant, even petty. If Baker had not intervened, Speke and Grant would have rejoiced at seeing Petherick's boats still waiting at Gondokoro loaded with supplies when they arrived. Instead of acting as peacemaker, as might have been expected, Baker fuelled the row by telling Speke about the £1,000 to fund the relief expedition raised by public subscription, including £100 donated by his own family. Speke's response was to accuse Petherick of the misappropriation of public funds. 'My heart filled with bitterness,' Katherine wrote to her sister. 'It seems incredible that he should impugn the honour and integrity of Petherick.' According to Petherick's own calculations the expedition had cost him four times that amount – and all to no avail. Speke announced he was accepting Baker's offer of transport down the Nile to Khartoum. Katherine pleaded with him to change his mind, the explorer replying coldly across his plate of preserved ham, but loud enough for all to hear, 'I do not wish to recognize the succour dodge and friend Baker has offered me his boats.' With this he lit a fire that consumed Petherick for the rest of his life. The conversation was hostile and recriminatory, upsetting Katherine so much that she was quite unable later to repeat it to anyone, not even to her greatest confidant, her sister Mona. All she would say was, 'Never mind, it will recoil upon him yet, his heartless conduct.' After that she left the table and never dined with Speke, Baker and Grant again.[14]

Speke's attitude hardened against the 'succour dodge,' the words a rapier thrust Petherick was unable to parry. Petherick's immediate response is not known although the Welshman would in time publish a passionate and detailed refutation of all allegations. In answer to Speke's charge that he failed to provide proper support for the expedition because he was too busy trading, Petherick eventually replied:

> He accuses me of trading at the Neambara … But it was true that I had been trading … was it not in this connection therewith that I first became known to the Royal Geographical Society? And was it not in accordance therewith that this very expedition was planned? And had Captain Speke forgotten his letter to me from 'Jordans'

dated 22 December 1859 wherein he suggested that geography and trade might be combined.

The impression conveyed to the public must be that I not only neglected my duty to the Speke Expedition in pursuit of my own interests, but with respect to the £1,000 contributed I made no use of it for that purpose, rendered no services, nor made any return whatever for it.

The Speke Expedition had no right to expect more than two boats and men to await them with supplies at Gondokoro. Instead of two, they found four awaiting them, one of which had been there for that purpose upwards of four months previous to their advent to that place, and the four were there eight months beyond the term June 1862, after which I was no longer bound to provide them.[15]

Katherine made one last attempt to make peace. The confrontation had precipitated another bout of fever but dragging herself from her sick bed the next morning she begged the man she saw as the principal troublemaker – Baker – to withdraw his offer of boats to Speke:

Mr Baker well knew the peculiar position Petherick held, and he was also aware that our boats had arrived prior to his. Mr Baker replied, 'Oh, Mrs Petherick, it will be a positive service to me if he [Speke] goes to Khartoum in one of my boats, as the men are paid in advance and his will serve as escort and guard.[16]

Tearfully, she pleaded with Baker to allow Petherick at least to provide the explorers with grain and stores for the journey. To this he reluctantly agreed. Hurrying back to the *Kathleen* she found Petherick too sick to move, but orders were given for everything the explorers needed, including wine and *araki*, to be packed in baskets. The baskets were returned unopened, with a note from Speke: 'All the articles enumerated have been packed by my friend Baker.' Such was the rift that Petherick's conditioned worsened. That he had not perished sooner was astonishing in a land where the tribute paid by Europeans was quick and painful, the majority breathing their last after less than a year's residency. By now Petherick had survived sixteen years! The dreaded ague would not kill him, not yet, but it was left to Katherine to wish Speke and Grant 'God speed' when they set off in Baker's boat for Khartoum. To the very end the explorers were unfriendly and uncooperative, to the extent of neglecting Katherine's request that on reaching England they tell her family that she and her husband were alive and on their way home.

In England, Speke's campaign of vilification was remorseless, the more surprising in view of the excessively cordial letter he left for Petherick while passing through Khartoum. Dated 15 April 1863, the day before he and Grant continued down the Nile to Alexandria and home, the letter, in which he thanks Petherick for use of the Consulate and his housekeeper 'the fair Fatima', was the last contact he would ever have with the Welshman. No mention is made of the 'succour dodge', Speke appearing either to have forgotten the incident or decided to ignore it:

> I was sorry to find on arrival here that the townspeople had reported you dead, and in consequence of it the Royal Geographical Society had determined on sending the second thousand pounds to Baker, with a view to assist him in looking after us. That now was too bad, for Hhalil [Petherick's Arab agent at Khartoum] never gave the slightest credence to the report brought down by the merchants, and said so in answer to his brother's inquiries concerning it at Cairo.
>
> To make the best of the matter, and to do justice to all, I wrote home a full explanation of our conversation at home before we left England, and the position in which we met at Gondokoro. Should you feel inclined to write a full statement of the difficulties you had to contend with in going up the White Nile, it would be a great relief to the mind of every person connected with the succouring funds, and also to myself *as the peoples' tongues are always busy in this meddling world* [author's italics].
>
> With Grant's best wishes, conjointly with my own, to Mrs Petherick and yourself, for your health and safety in the far interior ...[17]

This display of cordiality vanished the moment Speke arrived home causing his critics to wonder whether his judgment was impaired by his epic journey. The family had some history of mental instability, and it seemed to Baker that Speke was the more exhausted of the two men. Others detected a 'haunted look' as the unforgiving explorer pursued Petherick relentlessly – and demanded the return of the £100 his family contributed towards the cost of the abortive rescue mission. He should also be made to refund every penny of the £1,000 subscribed by well-wishers, Speke told the Royal Geographical Society. Before catching the boat from Alexandria to England, Speke spoke to the British Consul-General Colquhoun of his suspicions, portraying the Welshman as not only negligent but as a thieving slave trader. Soon afterwards on 4 June 1863 Colquhoun advised Austen Layard, Permanent Under-Secretary at the Foreign Office that it appeared as though

Petherick was dabbling in the slave trade. Under the heading 'The State of Khartoum' Colquhoun suggested to the home government a review of the consulate at Khartoum. 'The consul should be above the reach of anything approaching to a suspicion of tampering in scenes such as Captain Speke describes,' advised Colquhoun.

The moment this was drawn to the Foreign Secretary's attention, Lord John Russell sacked Petherick as though he was a felon and without the opportunity to answer the allegations. No customary thanks for years of loyal service: only that the Consulate was being abolished because the Foreign Office no longer required one at Khartoum to serve the public interest. Petherick was told to pack up and get out:

> I have accordingly to state to you that on and after the 1st February next your functions as her Majesty's Consul for the Sudan will be at an end. You will on termination of your services under this department, seal up and deliver to Her Majesty's Agent and Consul-General at Alexandria the whole of your official archives.[18]

The closure of the British Consulate was not such a good idea, according to Eugène de Pruyssenaere, a Belgian living in Khartoum. In a letter published by the *Athenaeum* on 9 April 1864 de Pruyssenaere – admittedly a friend of Petherick's – drew appropriate attention to the fact that if the British Government had sufficient reason to establish a Consulate in 1849, there was now an even more powerful case for one. 'Every year one hundred vessels leave Khartoum for the purpose of hunting down the natives; and slaves, who were formerly brought in by stealth, are now dragged publicly along the highways of the country, and even through the streets of Khartoum with a yoke upon their necks,' he said. Petherick had tried to stop this but because most Khartoumers lived by slave trading his reputation was destroyed, and his superiors failed to back him, the Belgian adding: 'The non-success of Mr Petherick in his proceedings against certain persons accused of this traffic has given license to these slave traders, and assured, henceforth, of impunity they have thrown off the mask ...'

Petherick blamed his dismissal on 'the treacherous behaviour of a *friend* ... who had without the slightest provocation or foundation so thoroughly poisoned the minds of the authorities.' It would be two years before he could attempt to answer the charges. In the meantime, no one doubted Speke's version of events to the extent that Lord Russell asked him to recommend a trustworthy person the Foreign Office could send to Khartoum to close the Consulate.

But Speke still had his critics, not least of all Burton who, ignoring Speke's almost universal acclaim continued to challenge the man celebrated for discovering the fountains of the Nile. Burton's case was that by failing to follow the course of the river flowing over the Ripon Falls from Victoria Nyanza Speke could not be certain it was the beginning of the White Nile. Another great lake 150 miles north-west could just as easily be the source. Speke had heard of the lake, Albert Nyanza but while at Rumanika's kraal never bothered to investigate although it was only ten days march away. But he did give Baker a map, ignoring Petherick for whom the undiscovered lake was also unfinished business having on a previous expedition reached within one hundred miles of it at Latitude 3° 40 N. Armed with Speke's directions, Baker would a year later discover and name Albert Nyanza in memory of Queen Victoria's consort Prince Albert of Saxe-Coburg and Gotha.

Reluctant to return to Britain empty-handed, mere footnotes to Speke's triumph, the Bakers and Pethericks, despite their differences, considered pooling resources for a joint assault upon Albert Nyanza. But the feeling against Petherick was so hostile that the idea was abandoned after Baker's men refused to go any further if accompanied by the former Consul, leaving the Pethericks no alternative but retreat to Khartoum while the Bakers pressed on alone.

Both had suffered recurring bouts of fever since reaching Gondokoro, Katherine at times too ill to lift her head off the pillow. Meanwhile, Arab mercenaries stalked the riverbank, aiming the occasional musket round in the direction of the *Kathleen* and fatally wounding their cabin boy. Would they be next? Petherick could barely reach his rifle. Dr Murie did what he could to make the couple comfortable but feared for Katherine especially. Weakened by fever and dysentery, she was nervous and confused, her mind wandering aimlessly. Dr Murie knew they would all die unless they escaped from Gondokoro, the struggle to stay alive more pressing than thoughts of further exploration.

Petherick was a broken man, flayed by vicious accusations, his affairs in ruins, their lives in constant danger. Unable to walk unaided, and his wife close to death, their situation was precarious. Before leaving, Speke had callously refused them a few bags of grain from Baker's stock. Dr Murie, their only ally, wrote to Katherine's brother-in-law Peter McQuie to warn that her condition was desperate:

> After nearly a year's journey from Khartoum to this place (which ordinarily is made in a couple to three months), with losses, disasters and difficulties daily befalling us, we arrived only to learn that,

from the Consul's activity in reporting and seizing those connected with the slave trade, he had drawn upon himself the hatred and vengeance of all the Arab traders and soldiers; but who, it seems, were really instigated by the intrigues of the Europeans of Khartoum, chiefly low rascally Frenchmen and Italians.

So great has the furore become against him that his life is not safe, his own and the other Arab soldiers when drunk coming and firing their guns close to the boat, showing, as they say, their defiance of him; at any moment a false shot may carry him off.[19]

What Katherine needed was 'a little calm and quiet'. Murie suspected a nervous breakdown. As for Petherick, the doctor believed he had been abandoned to his fate by a British Government asking him to suppress slavery yet failing to provide adequate support:

What I fear is that after all his outlay, and the losses and suffering he has undergone, that he will get but little credit for it from those at home, Captain Speke having come right on, and almost refusing him aid ... Khartoum is a hotbed of enemies, so that no Arab soldier will enter his service: this being the case, Mr Petherick is all but ruined, and I see nothing before him but to return to Europe ...[20]

Before leaving for Albert Nyanza, Baker extracted a promise from Petherick to dispatch the *Kathleen* with supplies back to Gondokoro to await their return. On 28 March 1863 the Welshman weighed down by fever single-handedly dragged the *Kathleen* into the current. Desertions and deaths left him with only three armed guards to fend off hostile natives while forcing a passage through the Sudd. The ill-fated journey would soon claim another victim: Foxcroft, the young botanist, weakened by recurring bouts of fever.

The dreary, featureless marshes of the Sudd were again the greatest obstacle, the course of the river barely visible amongst the reeds. Mornings were intensely cold and damp; by midday the heat was oppressive; and at dusk the mosquitoes were merciless. On 12 April they reached the lagoon where some of their canoes were sunk the previous year, after which Petherick had taken the disastrous decision to travel overland to Gondokoro. The chief who led that attack boarded the *Kathleen* to apologise, and to explain the terrible retribution his tribe had suffered. Four elephant rifles were salvaged from the sunken canoes, but not knowing what they were, the natives knocked off the stocks and took the barrels to a local blacksmith to be converted into lances unaware they were loaded, the powder and buckshot exploding in the forge killing several bystanders.[21]

By the middle of the month Petherick was strong enough to shoot game for the pot and Katherine to resume her journal. A Nuer man, she noted, could have as many wives as he pleased, the wealthiest fifty or more, each in a separate hut. The dead were buried in the immediate vicinity to prevent corpses being exhumed and eaten by other tribes. A person dying of small-pox was thrown in the Nile and those killed in battle left on the field to rot. The Nuer believed in neither a God, afterlife, nor good or evil spirits, only that they were visited by their dead.

Remarkably, near the White Nile's confluence with the Bahr al-Ghazal, the Pethericks stumbled upon the Tinné expedition. Unable to proceed beyond the rapids at Gondokoro, the Dutch family's steamboat had returned safely to Khartoum and after repairs was heading for the Bahr al-Ghazal on the first stage of a journey to Lake Chad. Alexine was accompanied by her mother Harriet, two European servants, a horse and donkeys, the steam-boat stopping twice a day to exercise their five dogs. A third member of the Tinné family, Harriet's sister Adriana von Capellan had chosen to remain in Khartoum. On hearing that the Pethericks were missing feared dead, the Tinnés had offered to deliver food and medicine to Gondokoro for Speke and Grant but, unlike Baker, resumed their own explorations when it was known the Pethericks were safe and travelling overland, and that relief boats and supplies were already awaiting the arrival of the missing explorers.

Progress from the mouth of the Bahr al-Ghazal was pitifully slow, the river no more than a muddy ditch. Firewood was scarce, provisions running low and the men restive, Katherine noting in her journal:

> The smallest possible passage through which the boat is dragged; some of the men using freely the knife and hatchet to cut away the ambage [sic] sweeping the decks, whilst others are overboard at the side of the *dahabyeh*, pushing her on; in the meanwhile from the decks no water can be seen, but apparently a vast meadow of rank high grass. Timing the tedious progress, we find one hundred yards is made in an hour and a half; this is the average.[22]

Petherick was surprised that so much had changed since his last visit when there were clear passages, some sixty yards wide, between the islands of rank weeds. Apart from two or three large pools, there were now only stag-nant ditches containing barely sufficient water to propel the *Kathleen* along by hand.

The *Kathleen* was preparing to moor beside a native village when one of their men waded through the swamp to warn that the village was crowded with slave boats; and the Pethericks were not welcome. It was while searching for an alternative mooring they came across the Tinnés: camped and waiting for their steamboat to return from Khartoum with fresh supplies and men to replace those who deserted. In the meantime, they had started overland across the savannah but were forced to pitch camp and wait when fierce storms swept across the marshes.

The chance encounter was a rare opportunity. The Pethericks dragged their dinghy through the swamp for an hour to reach the Tinnés' camp:

> Warmly were we welcomed by the beautiful Miss Tinné, who introduced us to her mother, truly a noble dame. With tact and delicacy the ladies gleaned from me that I was ignorant of our having been mourned for as dead. Though Mr Baker mentioned there were vague reports to that effect, he had treated them lightly; but now Madame Tinné showed extracts from newspapers asserting that we were no more. Oh, how I wept! Well knowing the pain such tidings must have inflicted upon those who loved us.[23]

Alexine and her companions were in desperate straits. Their native porters had bolted; the German botanist Dr Hermann Steudner was dead, the German ornithologist Baron Theodor von Heuglin was too sick to move, and while awaiting the return of Baron d'Ablaing and the steamboat from Khartoum, their guards mutinied. Alexine stood her ground until they laid down their weapons.

Before the Pethericks could return to their boat, Katherine collapsed again, her husband lifting her in his arms and carrying her through the swamp to the *Kathleen*. Unless they escaped the fetid marsh she would die, warned Dr Murie. Slowly, and with brute force, the boat was dragged out of the suffocating vegetation into the main current. Katherine recovered and for a time the *Kathleen* was carried quickly downstream until a strong wind blowing from the north slowed progress again. On entering a stretch of open water that Nile traders called 'the Pond', five boats were spotted moored to the bank, flying the Ottoman flag, and loading slaves. The Pethericks landed to take a closer look but as soon as they were spotted the able-bodied slaves were driven into the woods leaving behind only those powerless to move, the women, children and the sick, their faces horribly scarred by smallpox. The children were mere skeletons, sad entreating eyes more eloquent than speech, their hands outstretched pleading for Katherine's help. The slave hunters, Baggara Arab horsemen crowded around menacingly forcing the Pethericks to retreat to the *Kathleen* where on the river's edge lay an emaciated native. 'Never can I forget the piteous sight,' Katherine wrote. 'Deaf ears were turned to my entreaties to rescue him; he had gone there to die.'

The Pethericks reached Khartoum on 15 June 1863, two and a half months after leaving Gondokoro, to find their credit stopped by local tradesmen and their stock of ivory stolen and sold for a fraction of its real value on the assumption they were dead. Drained of energy, reputation destroyed, and business ruined, it seemed to Katherine her husband had lost all hope.

After weeks of waiting, a bagful of mail arrived from England. His hands trembling, Petherick cut open the bag, then turning to his wife said sadly, 'Be a brave girl, this is Baker's post.' Unable to handle another disappointment, Katherine fainted, not regaining consciousness until the next morning. Dozens of letters were scattered across her bed. Their post had, indeed, arrived and the first letter opened was from her mother containing a lock of golden hair and news that Katherine's daughter Frances had married. It took two days to read everything. From all accounts, Speke was continuing to vilify the Welshman, impugning his honour and integrity, he powerless to defend himself against the smears.

Life was precarious. Between recurring bouts of fever they scanned the river for the *Kathleen* which, as promised, had returned immediately to Gondokoro to collect the Bakers. Without the boat they were trapped in Khartoum, too sick to attempt the journey by camel across the Nubian Desert to Korosko below the second cataract.[24]

Through all their troubles, Katherine's steadfast support and dedication shines through, never once faltering or doubting her husband. 'Do not grieve,' she assured her sister after receiving a batch of damaging newspaper cuttings, 'all will end well; Petherick will see Speke upon our return. Wait the result patiently: we have no fear … Petherick must be in his place again: there has been nothing to conceal, no action to blush for, no wrong done to anyone, and right will come right.'[25]

On the evidence of Katherine's diaries Petherick was caring and considerate, her only criticism that he thought others as virtuous as himself. If anyone was at fault it was she for asking too much. 'Peth grieves to see the weak state I am in,' she wrote. 'At times I am very petulant and he is so patient and forbearing.'[26] But had she seen only one side of a man who is not easy to define? The account of their *Travels in Central Africa* is mostly hers. Only when she is too ill to write does her husband take up the narrative, but reveals almost nothing about Petherick the adventurer and White Nile trader.

The long wait for the *Kathleen* and the Bakers dragged on. Hopes rose after some boats were sighted approaching Khartoum, but dashed when the Dutch flag was seen flying from their masts. They were returning from the Bahr al-Ghazal after delivering provisions to the Tinnés at the start of their overland trek to Lake Chad. Unknown to the Tinnés, their Arab crews had filled the empty holds with another cargo – slaves smuggled under the protection of the Dutch flag. 'This is a horrible place,' wrote Katherine to her sister on being told that the Khartoum traders were insinuating that 'all the Europeans traffic in slaves, even the Dutch ladies.' You cannot imagine, she wrote, the atrocities taking place. 'Whole batches of Negroes are marched to the Government quarters, and even the dead and dying are thither dragged, that the captured may be duly accounted for.'[27]

As the year wore on, concern for the safety of the Tinnés grew. Adriana von Capellan wasted away waiting anxiously for news of her sister Harriet and niece Alexine. Hopes were frequently raised then dashed, and with Miss von Capellan's health failing, the Pethericks resolved to take her with them to Alexandria when eventually the *Kathleen* returned. In March 1864 Katherine wrote to her sister joyously but prematurely, 'We are going home!' The next leg of the journey would not be by boat as she hoped but by dromedaries across the dreaded Nubian Desert again. When an outbreak of smallpox swept through Khartoum they fled into the desert to camp beside the river seven miles away.

In April the khamsin blew a suffocating, blinding wall of sand off the desert into the camp, the hot blast pushing the temperature to 112° F (44° C). One night a watchman, posted to raise the alarm if the *Kathleen* was sighted, was heard hailing a passing boat. In the moonlight the Pethericks saw a dahabeeyah being hauled ashore – but not the *Kathleen*. Aboard were Baron d'Ablaing and Baron von Heuglin, the Tinnés' two surviving male companions. The news was bad. Alexine's mother perished the previous July, only a month after parting company with the Pethericks at the mouth of the Bahr al-Ghazal. In August, Alexine's favourite maid Flora died from typhoid as did the second European servant later.

The next morning the Pethericks rode into Khartoum to break the news to Miss von Capellan. On the river, Alexine's steamboat glided past with its melancholy cargo. Filled with grief and guilt, Alexine was returning her mother's body to Holland for burial in the family tomb in the Hague. But she would not accompany her; in fact, would never see Holland again. Family and friends held Alexine personally responsible for the tragedy.

Seven weeks later Alexine's aunt, Adriana von Capellan, also died, a wan and solitary figure whose grim determination was finally beaten by the tragic events. The day before, Miss von Capellan drew Katherine Petherick to one side and whispered, 'I must tell you my dreams. Last night I saw my lovely mother and my dead sister – the one next to me; they held out their arms from the bright clouds to take me there, and I was so happy. Then I awoke, but to sleep again and to dream of Harriet that she was dead.' The next day she developed a slight fever and died with Katherine at her bedside.[28]

The heat and dust of their desert camp, and the unrelenting wind was killing Katherine. Better, it was decided, to take their chances with smallpox in Khartoum until the khamsin abated, the rains came, and the Nubian Desert crossing was easier. In the meantime, another boat arrived from Gondokoro, not the *Kathleen*, but one carrying the corpse of Amabile de Bono, killed by a native lance. There was also news that the Bakers were expected in a matter of weeks. 'We have been anxious for his safety, though he has proved no friend,' wrote Katherine. 'The English heart clings to its kind, and we hope and trust he will turn up all right.'[29]

The *Kathleen* did arrive at the end of May 1864 but without the Bakers who were last reported close to their goal, Albert Nyanza. But with their quinine exhausted, it was a race against time to find the great lake before they also succumbed, Baker calculating that without quinine they had less than a year to live. Following the directions provided by Speke they reached the kraal of the native king Kamrasi who promised to lead them to the lake – but only if Baker gave him Florence! Surrounded by hundreds of spear-waving natives, Kamrasi waited expectantly. Baker resolved that if this were to be the end then it would be the end of Kamrasi, too:

Drawing my revolver quietly, I held it within two feet of his chest, and looking at him with undisguised contempt, I told him that if I touched the trigger not all his men could save him: and that if I dared to repeat the insult I would shoot him on the spot. At the same time I explained to him that in my country such insolence would entail bloodshed, and that I looked upon him as an ignorant ox who knew no better ... My wife [they were not married until the following year] naturally indignant had risen from her seat, and, maddened with the excitement of the moment, she made a little speech in Arabic (not a word of which Kamrasi understood), with a countenance almost as amiable as the head of Medusa ... Whether this little *coup de théâtre* had so impressed Kamrasi with British female independence he said, 'Don't be angry! I had no intention of offending you by asking for your wife; I will give you a wife, if you want one, and I thought you might have no objection to give me yours; it is my custom to give my visitors pretty wives, and I thought you might exchange. Don't make a fuss about it; if you don't like it there's an end to it; I will never mention it again.'[30]

With that, the Bakers were led to Albert Nyanza, sighting and naming another of the great Central African lakes on 14 March 1864. By the time they returned to Khartoum in May 1865, the Pethericks would be back in England.

Shaking with fever, Katherine Petherick managed a smile when on 5 July 1864 she boarded the *Kathleen*. They were going home, the *Kathleen* joining the sombre flotilla carrying the bodies of Harriet and Adriana Tinné to Cairo. Alexine's dahabeeyah led the way, followed by the barge with the coffins. For safety's sake they sailed together as far as Abu Hamad at which point Alexine hired camels to cross the desert to the Red Sea, then by steamer to Suez. Fed by rains in the Ethiopian Highlands, the Nile was in flood, the Pethericks increasingly hopeful the *Kathleen* could clear the cataracts below Abu Hamad, enabling them to avoid the desert crossing. But entering a rocky section, the boat was sucked into a whirlpool and thrown against large boulders, each splintering thud threatening to sink it. After scrambling ashore Katherine refused to travel any further by river. That left only the desert.

Most of their possessions were unloaded to lighten the *Kathleen* sufficiently to clear the rapids while for good luck the crew slaughtered a sheep, sprinkling its blood over the vessel's bow. The *Kathleen* would wait at Korosko until they emerged from the desert. But no sooner had the boat sailed and the Pethericks found themselves stranded – no one would hire them camels. Abu Hamad was not beyond the terrifying reach of the Sudanese Governor-General Moosa Pasha and his firman that the former British Consul should receive no assistance whatsoever. While Petherick searched for camels, Katherine lived like a prisoner in a stinking shed on the edge of the village. 'You cannot picture the wretched quarters,' she wrote to her sister. 'The heat is intolerable during the day and we are compelled to remain in this shed; light there is none, but that which creeps through the low portal; at night we sleep in the square or public streets where do all the travellers. It is a weird sight to open one's eyes and see the tall camels with their noiseless step march past ...' During frequent bouts of feverish hallucinations she imagined Petherick being bastinadoed (footwhipped). So real was the delirium that whenever he returned to the shed she examined the soles of his feet for bloody scars.[31]

Of the thirteen camels eventually mustered, some were wild. A litter was suspended between two dromedaries and in this swinging palanquin Petherick placed a mattress with pillows and above it an awning with wide curtains. Slipping in and out of consciousness Katherine dreamed always of a high wall blocking their path. The heat hung choking in the air. Alongside the trail, the bleached skeletons of dead camels poked like ghostly ridges through the thirsty sand. Once, on their approach, a spectre staggered to its feet, luminous eyes pleading for water as they passed on to the next well and their own salvation. Rain seldom touched the arid wrinkled sandstone of dried-up river valleys. When it did, it was swallowed by the desert before reaching the Nile. For hours they travelled, never resting, winding between rocky outcrops to avoid the slow-moving slave caravans, Katherine's heart filling with grief as she counted the tiny footprints of children in the sand. Unable to suffer the sickening motion of the litter any longer she mounted a dromedary but fell to the sand, pleading, 'Let me remain behind! I am dying.' In the moonlight, staring at a face as white as marble, Petherick feared she had, indeed, reached the end of their long and painful journey. While he comforted his wife, others were sent for water from a distant well only to return with a little milk purchased from some passing Bedouins. Next morning after a deep and restful sleep Katherine bravely remounted, testifying to a fortitude and resolution equal to her husband. Then, across a rocky ridge they saw the Nile glistening in the distance, the men rushing ahead to fetch water and handfuls of lemons for Katherine to suck on. Through the shimmering haze the crew of their dahabeeyah hurried out to welcome them. The *Kathleen* had survived the rapids. Soon she was gliding swiftly downstream, past the ruins at Luxor and on to Cairo.[32]

CHAPTER 10

A Very Public Quarrel

PEKE RETURNED TO A HERO'S WELCOME. Feted by the Viceroy before leaving Egypt, and presented with a medal bearing the gratifying inscription *Honor est a Nilo*, he was royally received at Southampton by the various civic authorities and sundry dignitaries – church bells ringing, thousands cheering as he drove in an open carriage through the town while the band played 'See, the Conquering Hero Comes'. His telegram with its immortal line 'the Nile is settled' paved the way for a rapturous reception, windows broken in an unseemly rush for seats when it was waved victoriously by Murchison before the Royal Geographical Society members on 11 May 1863. The fate of the Pethericks was forgotten in the clamour to hear Speke deliver his personal account.[1] His single-handed achievement – Grant already side-lined – gripped the imagination of a euphoric nation eager for sight of the intrepid explorer whose account of fraternizing with native women, as much as his feat of endurance, guaranteed that *The Discovery of the Source of the Nile* was an immediate best-seller among a Victorian readership unaccustomed to sexually explicit narrative. Others thought Speke should not have 'stained the pages with such rubbish' as speculating about the colour of his progeny if, indeed, he was tempted by the young virgins delivering water to his tent – or whatever else he chose to give them to carry, his old adversary Burton observed. 'Mbugu is a favourite word with our author [Speke],' wrote Burton. 'It occurs on almost every page. It is made of bark-cloth, of a shape as female fancy dictates. As far as we can gather [from] the meaning of the name, it signifies not to cover, but to show the part that should be covered.'[2]

Petherick would not leave Egypt for another four months while the Egyptian Government investigated the accusations of the Khartoum traders. In his absence, however, Burton sprang to his defence by publicly rebuking Speke and his sponsors at the Royal Geographical Society for the shoddy way they treated the Welshman. But was Burton's support intended, primarily, to cast further doubt over Speke's assertions about Victoria Nyanza than to defend Petherick? In fairness, Burton was equally scathing of the Foreign Office's role in the affair, especially the intervention of Consul-General Colquhoun who, he complained, had informed the Home Government of the allegations that Petherick was a slave trader without allowing him the right of reply. 'If he [Consul-General] did all this, then it is the Consul-General not the Consul who should be dismissed,' wrote Burton. In order that the British people should know the truth, a legislative inquiry with full access to all the papers and correspondence was necessary. How was it, Burton asked, that the Foreign Office permitted the ruin and oppression of a British subject by men infesting a 'horrid den … of chiefly low, rascally Frenchmen and Italians!' Burton had no doubt that Speke's 'unfounded charges' had influenced the British Government and that his 'flippant conduct and proceedings' was to blame for the ruin brought upon the Pethericks.[3] The Royal Geographical Society, he said, having recruited Petherick as the best man to support Speke, and then to transfer the mission to Baker without good enough reason, was partly responsible for the unfortunate outcome.

At first Murchison was content to share Speke's triumph. After all, it was he who sent Speke back to Africa to locate the point at which the Nile exited Victoria Nyanza. The possibility that proceedings might be taken against Petherick by the Egyptian Government only reinforced the Society's opinion that he was indeed the 'succour dodge'. Later, when the geographical establishment saw that Speke had left important questions still unanswered, Murchison moderated his support for Speke. Was it the Nile that he saw exiting Victoria Nyanza, or some other river? To help resolve this, the Society invited the contestants Speke and Burton to debate the rival merits of their candidates – Victoria Nyanza and Lake Tanganyika – before members at its meeting in Bath on 16 September 1864. At this Burton would not confine himself to exposing the geographical flaws in his rival's claim that Victoria Nyanza was the great reservoir feeding the Nile, but also use the moment to censure Speke for his uncorroborated and pitiless attacks upon Petherick. His speech to members – not delivered but published later – applauded the Welshman for his efforts, sympathised with his misfortunes, and berated his critics:

> … an individual whom Speke urged to join and aid him in his journey – the man the Foreign Office patronized, assisted, and permitted to lend his aid – an energetic and experienced individual whom the Royal Geographical Society, through their proper authorities,

encouraged, assisted, prompted, and selected as the most proper individual they could find to convey assistance and advice to Speke, now thrown overboard without pity, his private fortune wasted, the health of himself and his heroic and attached wife ... irretrievably ruined, and his character ... blasted in the eyes of his countrymen and of the civilized world by being charged with a dereliction of duty, and with the crime of slave dealing, at the moment he was doing everything in his power to put it down.[4]

Burton's criticism of Speke already had the support of some eminent members of the Society, in particular James McQueen, respected geographer who, as a long-standing opponent of Speke, had objected to him receiving the Society's Gold Medal award for achievement. By now, the explorer's irrationality was beginning to trouble Murchison. So intemperate was the denunciation of Petherick by Speke in some telegrams sent during a visit to Paris that Murchison refused to publish what he described as 'these aberrations'. At the same time, in a clumsy attempt to protect his favourite explorer, Murchison censored a letter from Petherick rebutting the charges before he allowed it to be published by the Welshman's brother-in-law Peter McQuie in the *Athenaeum*. The deleted sentences (below) would seem to suggest that Speke's mental faculties were impaired by his experiences, and that consumed by jealousy and spite his 'aberrations' had focused on Petherick. In censoring the letter, Murchison by denying Petherick the opportunity to clear his name allowed Speke's accusations to take deeper root. It would be another two years before the Welshman could put the record straight by which time it was virtually too late. The public would have been better informed about events if the following sentences about the Petherick-Speke meeting in Gondokoro had been published by the *Athenaeum*:

He would or could not understand the difficulties and sacrifices we had put ourselves to, to meet him; and having helped himself from our stores to sundry blue cloth and other indispensable necessaries for the clothing of his men prior to our arrival, he heaped insult to injury upon us by refusing our boats and provisions, preferring those of Mr Samuel Baker, then present, notwithstanding our representation that the whole had been paid for, and we were expected to supply him with every necessity. Grant was throughout *the gentleman*, but Speke I shall never forgive. Our engagement to meet him, he said, had virtually expired in June 1862, and he would now purchase any article he required. How indignantly this was refused you may imagine, but the crowning piece of all his ill-temper was the ignoring of my expedition, ending with the inquiry to whom he had proposed it! He was rather astonished at my *repartée* – that our meeting [at Gondokoro] was proposed by himself, and his letter to that effect was still, doubtless, preserved by the Council of the Geographical Society. His jealousy was so aggravated as to lead him to declare he required no succour dodge!

Although he had had ample experience of the violence, robbery, and slave kidnapping propensities of the traders to the aborigines, he was dumb upon the subject; but when I stated that – travelling through districts long ruined by them, and where the natives would not employ themselves as porters for anything short of a cow or bullock each, and that far in the interior we could neither return nor advance without them – our men had joined a party of traders in a *razzia* to supply us with the needful cattle, and restore some sixty head already borrowed from a trader for former Negro services, Speke would make no allowances for our peculiar circumstances or the alacrity of our men (although much against our will) to pay the Negroes out for former wanton assaults against ourselves; and I will not be surprised that Speke and Baker, hand in glove, will make some ill-natured remark on the subject at home. However, as nothing that has transpired will be withheld from the public, with a clear conscience I will willingly abide their decision.[5]

The Speke that Petherick knew was very different to the 'bold explorer, sagacious discoverer with a sunny smile' portrayed by William Blackwood, owner of *Blackwood's Magazine* and publisher of Speke's memoirs *The Discovery of the Source of the Nile*. Never envious but sweet tempered, amiable, and kindly towards everyone with whom he had contact, Speke was acquitted by *Blackwood's Magazine* of ever being disingenuous, the magazine adding, 'By the friendly hearth, in fact, he had so much good-humour, docility, and pliability about trifles, that people who saw no more of him might have formed the utterly mistaken notion that he was infirm of purpose, and wanting in the hardness of character necessary for great achievements.' The magazine dismissed Speke's critics as 'carpers and detractors'.[6]

His principal opponent, Burton, while not doubting what Speke endured to reach Victoria Nyanza thought his hardships might have been greatly reduced by 'common prudence and proper caution, good temper and patience', all qualities *Blackwood's Magazine* said its man had in abundance!

As for Speke's triumph, the *Westminster Review* asked how he could propose Victoria Nyanza for the final accolade when he had actually only seen two points, one in the north and the other in the south? The route taken by Speke and Grant ran parallel to Victoria Nyanza which Speke never saw on his final expedition until reaching Murchison Creek and afterwards the outlet at the Ripon Falls. As it happened, because of sickness Grant did not see the lake pouring out over the Ripon Falls although he never doubted Speke's word that it existed.[7]

The jury was still out, Speke's triumph battered by recrimination and backbiting. At Bath, Burton waited for the Royal Geographical Society confrontation to deliver the equivalent of a geographers' *coup de grâce*. In his opinion Speke was guessing at the source of the Nile – his map of the lakes region adding nothing that was not already known to the second century Alexandrian geographer Claudius Ptolemy. 'The less that is said about the map the better,' Burton sneered, adding, 'The publishers have furnished us with a really good book, as a book – good paper, clear and legible type together with many curious and well-executed sketches of Africans in their various and ludicrous attitudes and proceedings.' Nor was Burton impressed with Speke's description of a cluster of dirty huts as 'a village built on the most luxurious principles', of a murderer and thief as a 'king of kings', and a display of wanton savagery as a 'splendid court'. The time Speke spent drinking native beer and flirting with Rumanika's fat wives and daughters might, Burton suggested, have been more usefully employed plotting the course of the unknown river exiting Victoria Nyanza seven miles from where he was being regally entertained to drunken orgies and to public executions. What deeply wounded Burton was Speke's speech at a commemorative dinner in Taunton at which he rasped triumphantly that he 'had in 1857 hit the Nile on the head and in 1863 drove it down to the Mediterranean'. On the same occasion Speke hammered another nail into Petherick's reputation by alleging publicly that 'men with authority emanating from our Government' were engaged in the diabolical slave trade.[8]

Petherick was pulling Guinea worms out of his leg when he read about this in the *Overland Mail* on Christmas Eve 1863. He resolved immediately to sue Speke for slander the moment he returned to Britain. 'The blow was as hard as I could well bear,' he wrote later. 'Therefore, in accordance with the advice of friends at home, and considering the distance I was from the scene of action to answer through the press, I decided, in lieu thereof, at a future date to enter proceedings against Captain Speke.'

Burton was waiting to deliver his masterly but cruel demolition at Bath when a single gunshot rescued Speke's floundering reputation. Speke was dead – killed, so it seemed, during a hunting accident in Somerset on the eve of the debate.

The last time Burton saw him was at the Mineral Water Hospital in Bath on 15 September 1864 at the business meeting preceding the Society's summer conference starting the following day with the presentations of the warring explorers. Burton's wife Isabel recalled that she and her husband sat quite close to Speke:

> He looked at Richard, and at me, and we at him. I shall never forget his face. It was full of sorrow, of yearning, and perplexity. Then he seemed turned to stone. After a while he began to fidget a great deal, and exclaimed half aloud, 'Oh, I cannot stand this any longer.' He got up to go out. The man nearest him said, 'Shall you want your chair again, Sir? May I have it? Shall you come back?' and he answered, 'I hope not' and left the hall.[9]

That was at 1 p.m. Three hours later Speke was lying dead in a field: his implacable and formidable rival Burton denied his moment, and Petherick his day in court. Without Speke's retraction the smears were bound to stick.

At home, the allegations of slave trading were as serious, if not more damaging to Petherick than the spat over whether or not he provided the Speke Expedition with the promised support, which was easy enough to rebut by reference to the correspondence and contract existing between the Welshman and Royal Geographical Society. The instructions were quite clear and, at first sight, seemed to have been followed to the letter (see appendix). Whatever interpretation the Society later chose to put upon the small print, the fact remained that the contract expired long before Speke and Grant reached at Gondokoro. But there was more at stake than the letter of the contract. Petherick was claiming reimbursement from the Society for hundreds of thousands of pounds (at 2005 values) of additional expenditure.

It is generally agreed that Petherick's greatest mistake as an experienced White Nile trader was to leave Khartoum for Gondokoro too late in the season. This, and the inexplicable decision to abandon his boats when only 150 miles from his destination and take Katherine overland on a journey few Europeans, let alone a woman, had ever attempted was unwise, and almost cost them their lives. But the commitment to Speke and Grant was not jeopardised by this. Petherick's boats were still waiting when they reached Gondokoro many months after the agreed dates for the rendezvous. Frankly, it was immaterial that before Speke and Grant reached Gondokoro the boats were briefly commandeered by Petherick's agent Majid to transport slaves. The Royal Geographical Society would, however, use this as proof that the Welshman was in breach of contract. The intervention of Baker, however, did muddy the waters and while the Royal Geographical Society cannot be criticised for mounting a rescue mission, it did so without any accurate knowledge of what had happened to the Pethericks. It was true they were not at Gondokoro – but neither were Speke and Grant. Speke's unreasonable reaction reflects somewhat on the authenticity of other parts of the account of a journey for which for long periods there were no witnesses, not even Grant. But his premature death resurrected, at least for a time, his fading credibility, leaving the allegations against Petherick still standing.

Burton was fiddling with the pages of the paper he was about to deliver to the Society's Bath conference when Murchison stunned members by announcing Speke's death. Burton sank into his chair, wrote his wife, 'and I saw by the workings of his face the terrible emotion he was controlling, and the shock he had received ... when we got home he wept long and bitterly, and I was for many a day trying to comfort him.'[10] The fatal shooting silenced many critics, some like David Livingstone revising their opinion. Having written earlier that 'poor Speke has turned his back upon the real source of the Nile ... his river at Ripon Falls is not long enough,' Livingstone now conceded that Speke was undoubtedly the discoverer of the source of the Nile, according to Grant after a conversation with Livingstone at Speke's funeral. Perhaps the missionary explorer was speaking kindly of the deceased because a year later he led his own expedition from Zanzibar to search for the source of the Nile which he continued to believe was further south than Victoria Nyanza. To help fund this, Livingstone received a donation of £2,000 from Speke's family – proceeds from sales of Speke's *Journal*, which soared following the accident.[11]

Not surprisingly, the public was intrigued to discover if it really was an accident, not suicide as some thought. A slew of speculation swirled around the incident, Speke's detractors convinced that in a fit of depression he shot himself to escape Burton, intellectually superior and about to expose his fraudulent claims about the Nile. Speke was no match for Burton, and was visibly nervous in the presence of the older, more experienced man. In addition, how could Speke substantiate his wild accusations about Petherick's slave trafficking, based as they were upon the testimony of a generally discredited group of 'Khartoum scum'? Petherick had resolved to sue, the only obstacle to his day in court a serious shortage of funds. But he had influential supporters besides Burton. James McQueen may never have set foot in Africa, but was highly regarded and collaborated with Burton in publishing *The Nile Basin* attack upon Speke's competence. From his home in Liverpool, Petherick's wealthy account-ant brother-in-law Peter McQuie had also mounted a vigorous defence through the columns of the *Times*. 'The calumny is so utterly absurd that he [Petherick] waits with impatience to be formally accused,' Katherine wrote to her sister. Was Speke anxious about facing Petherick in court? Was this yet another consideration pressing on his mind alongside the forthcoming confrontation with Burton when his shotgun discharged into his chest on 15 September 1864 severing the main artery?

The Speke inquest was, to say the least, precipitous, held the next day at Mont's Park, Wiltshire, the home of his brother William Speke, the jury composed of 'respectable inhabitants of the place', according to the *Times*. Evidence of it being an accident rather than deliberate was flimsy, providing fertile ground for suicide theorists ever since.

The shooting occurred at Neston Park, Corsham, Wiltshire home of Speke's cousin, George Fuller, heir to the London brewing family. There were only two witnesses, George Fuller and his gamekeeper Daniel Davis. A surgeon named Snow gave evidence of cause of death, after which the Coroner, Mr Kemm, directed the jury to return a verdict that 'the deceased died from the accidental discharge of his own gun after living a quarter of an hour'. What puzzled most people was how a widely experienced big game hunter in Asia and Africa, a man with a great passion for guns succeeded in killing himself accidentally in a field in Wiltshire while shooting par-tridge? Was he preoccupied, perhaps with Burton and Petherick, or simply negligent, carelessly disregarding the half-cocked shotgun in his hand as he stepped across a low, crumbling stone wall from one field into the next? Because of the various extrapolations, the scant evidence is given here *in extenso* as reported in the *Times*:

George Fuller, son of Mr Fuller of Neston Park:

About half past 2 o'clock yesterday I left my father's house for the purpose of shooting partridges. Deceased had fired off both barrels before the accident occurred. About 4 o'clock I got over a low part of a loose stone wall at that place about two feet high and I was about 60 yards from the place when I heard the report of a gun and looking round thinking to see some birds I saw the deceased standing on the same part of the wall I had just got over without his gun and shortly after I saw him fall into the field I was then in. I immediately went to his assistance and found a wound in his chest bleeding, which I endeavoured to stop. He was then sensible and spoke to me but did not long remain so. I stayed with him about five minutes and then left him in charge of my keeper Daniel Davis and went for assistance. I observed the gun lying by the side of the wall in the field that I and the deceased were in. One barrel, the right, was then at half cock, the left hand barrel was discharged. I heard very little report and I should suppose that the muzzle of the gun was very near the body of the deceased when it went off.

Daniel Davis, keeper to Mr Fuller:

> Yesterday a little before 4 o'clock I was marking birds for my master and the deceased who were shooting. At that time I saw the deceased go up to a low part of the wall to get over. He had then his gun in his hand. Almost immediately after I heard the report of a gun and I looked towards my master and on seeing him running towards the deceased I went there also. He was then lying by the side of the wall he had just got over. I found him with a wound in his side and Mr Fuller had his hand on the wound trying to stop the blood. I heard the deceased groan once or twice but cannot say whether he was actually sensible or not. I stayed with him until he died which was about a quarter of an hour after the gun was discharged. He was not removed from the spot before he died. The gun was a Lancaster breach-loader, without safety guard but I should think the gun was quite safe and in the same state as gentlemen's guns usually are.

Mr Thomas Fitzherbert Snow, surgeon of Box:

> There was a wound on the left side, such as would be made by a cartridge if the muzzle of the gun was close to the body. There was no other wound. It led in a direction upwards and towards the spine passing through the lungs and dividing all the large blood vessels near the heart but not touching the heart itself. Such a wound would cause death.

Forty years later when George Fuller was an old man he wrote a more detailed account for the Speke family corroborating the inquest verdict and rebutting the suggestion Speke committed suicide rather than face Burton. 'Hanning was a traveller as a sportsman in search of game; Burton was a traveller as an author in search of a reputation,' he said.[12] The statement is confused, Fuller insisting the accident was on 1 September not 15 September and that Speke never attended the preliminary meeting of the Royal Geographical Society in Bath when he was plainly seen by dozens. The only material difference from the inquest is that Fuller said Speke was carrying his shotgun by the muzzle, which might better explain the direction of the fatal shot, but made suicide well-nigh impossible because unless he was a contortionist he could not have reached the trigger. This was not mentioned at the inquest, nor did the surgeon find any other wound which might have been expected if Speke was holding the muzzle when the gun discharged. On balance, the more credible explanation is that he either lost his balance crossing the ruined wall, or that a loose stone jutting from it, even a piece of vegetation, triggered the fatal shot.

After the accident Burton wrote to an associate in Fernando Po where he was about to be appointed British Consul that 'the charitable say that he shot himself, the uncharitable that I shot him'.[13] In the circumstances, the Royal Geographical Society might have expected Burton as a mark of respect for his former partner to postpone what amounted to a cruel attack on the dead man's reputation. But within two months of Speke's death, members were invited to hear Burton's critique, unchanged from what he was preparing to deliver in Bath, apart from an introductory chapter explaining his precipitousness. He said in justification:

> I cannot do justice to the public, as well as to myself, allow errors – of late almost generally received – to make further way. At the same time, be it distinctly understood that whilst differing from Captain Speke upon almost every geographical subject supposed to be 'settled' by his exploration of 1860–1863, I do not stand forth as an enemy of the departed; that no man better appreciate the noble qualities of energy, courage, and perseverance which he so eminently possessed than I do, who knew him for so many years, and who travelled with him as a brother, until the unfortunate rivalry respecting the Nile Sources arose like the ghost of discord between us, and was fanned to a flame by the enmity and ambition of 'friends'. ... It is now, I believe, the opinion of scientific Europe that the problem is wholly unsolved, and, more still, that within the last four years the Nile Basin has acquired an amount of fable which it never had in the days of Pliny and Ptolemy.

Burton persisted in delivering a withering criticism of Speke as an explorer and geographer. 'A lake,' he said, 'unless it be a mere "eye" of water cannot be taken as the head of a river, though the river may issue from it … Lake Tana is not the head of the Blue Nile … Lake Geneva is not the head of the Rhône … Lake Superior not the head of the St Lawrence.' Burton concluded by saying that the 'great Nile problem' rather than being 'settled for ever' had become even more difficult to resolve because of the Speke Expedition. 'The exploratory labours of years, of perhaps a whole generation, must be lavished before even a rough survey of the southern Nilotic basin can treat the subject with approximate correctness of detail,' Burton said.[14]

But he was wrong. What he thought was a guess by Speke proved to be correct when Samuel Baker and his wife Florence discovered that the river exiting Victoria Nyanza at the Ripon Falls did indeed flow into Albert Nyanza from which it become the Mountain Nile at the start of a 4,000-mile (6,650 kilometres) journey to the Mediterranean. Three million years earlier Burton could have been right – before a shift in the African tectonic plate threw up the Virunga Volcanoes separating Tanganyika from Albert Nyanza. Before this cataclysm, the Nile was 870 miles longer and its source was one of the distant tributaries of Tanganyika. Since then the waters of Tanganyika instead of flowing north into the Mediterranean had turned westwards into the Congo River basin. Nevertheless, but for a mere one hundred miles Tanganyika, the second deepest lake in the world, could have been Burton's Nile reservoir. As it happens the true source of the Nile – as opposed to its reservoirs Victoria Nyanza and Albert Nyanza – was not finally discovered until the early 21st century bubbling from the ground in the mountains of what is now the Republic of Burundi between lakes Tanganyika and Victoria.

CHAPTER 11

Unfinished Business

THE PETHERICKS WERE RESTING AT ASWAN aboard the *Kathleen* en route to Cairo when Katherine read an account of Speke's death in a back issue of an English newspaper. 'Almost the first paragraph which attracted my attention was the one relating to the awfully sudden death of Captain Speke,' Katherine wrote to her sister Mona. 'For his untimely end sorrow came over me like some tremendous wave, sweeping away the bitterness which had filled my heart against him. Petherick, utterly subdued, spoke tenderly of the man he had once deemed a friend.'[1]

The next morning, perhaps in reaction to the news, Katherine was delirious and it would be several days before she was able to continue on to Cairo, arriving there on 25 November 1864. With the *Kathleen* safely moored off the island of Roda opposite old Cairo, Katherine's spirits were revived by the mountain of letters awaiting them. Petherick still had friends and supporters. The eminent geographer James McQueen had accused Speke of indulging in an orgy of licentious living while at Rumanika's palace, and had also joined with Burton in censuring Speke for the slanders perpetrated against Petherick. The Welshman replied immediately thanking both for their generous support and for daring to risk the disfavour of Speke's adoring supporters, and in the aftermath of his death, a sympathetic public. 'It will not be an easy and highly cherished task,' he wrote, 'to convince them that I was not unworthy of their support, during absence, in peril, and through evil and false report.'[2] In England, prior to Speke's tragic accident, Petherick's brother-in-law Peter McQuie wrote to the *Times* repudiating Speke's description of the slave traffickers at Falaro as 'Petherick's Turks'. Petherick had no connection with their infamous traffic, said McQuie castigating Speke for ignoring the hardships suffered by the Pethericks. Not content, wrote McQuie, with casting aspersions upon the integrity and honour of Consul Petherick, Speke had insinuated he abandoned his mission in order to trade.[3] Four days later the *Times* published Speke's reply which repeated the charge that Petherick had left the Nile to trade when only 150 miles from Gondokoro. 'Illness, he says, prevented his doing so [providing succour] personally ... On meeting Mr Petherick at Gondokoro I did not conceal my feelings with regard to this matter ... speaking out plainly,' replied Speke.[4] The long-distance war of words continued through the columns of the newspaper, Speke stung into defending himself. Rounding on Petherick he insisted,

> He never gave me the least assistance in reaching Gondokoro. Mr de Bono [the teenage slave trader], a bitter rival in trade of Mr Petherick, which I did not know when I was in the interior, is the only person in the White Nile trade to whom the East African Expedition owes thanks. He did exactly that which Mr Petherick ought to have done when he sent his traders up the Nile and told them to look for our approach from the south. Had Mr de Bono's men not ... I should now be in that country ... and Grant on his way to England to organize another expedition. How many lives would have been sacrificed by this nobody knows, but the whole onus of it would have been on Mr Petherick's shoulders.[5]

Speke's campaign against Petherick continued beyond the grave! The day before he died in the unexplained hunting accident, Speke wrote to John Tinné, stepbrother of Alexine, and then living in Liverpool. The unfinished letter found among Speke's possessions after his death was subsequently sent to Mr Tinné and published in the *Times*. In this Speke said the suspicions that Nile traders had about 'prying foreigners' was a major obstacle to exploration in Central Africa. Then in a final dig at Petherick he added, 'No doubt, indeed, a Consul is much wanted in the Sudan; but then he should not be a trader, for no one can trade honestly in those regions.' In an explanatory footnote, Mr Tinné made it absolutely clear that he had no reason to suspect that the former British Consul was in any way concerned with the slave trade.[6]

Petherick waited in Cairo to be formally accused by the Egyptian Government. But after the deaths of Amabile de Bono and Speke it was unlikely that either the Egyptian or British governments, even if inclined, could muster sufficient evidence to proceed against him. The charges were not dropped, but he was allowed to leave Egypt in April 1865, four years after arriving for the epic expedition. Before sailing from Alexandria into the struggle to clear his name, he sold the last of his possessions, the redoubtable *Kathleen*.

Petherick's first move on arriving home was to ask the Foreign Office to investigate the slave trafficking allegations. Although there was never a formal investigation, the Foreign Secretary Lord Russell replied on 21 June 1865 saying there was 'no evidence before Her Majesty's Government that you had any direct participation in this traffic and Her Majesty's Government acquits you of any such participation'. But this fell short of complete exoneration, Russell having added the caveat that 'no trade on the White Nile, by Europeans or natives, was conducted without directly or indirectly encouraging the slave traffic'. Petherick was also reminded that slaves were found on his own boats, although the Government accepted this was without his knowledge or sanction. Russell's cautious endorsement of Petherick was on the advice of the Consul-General Colquhoun who in a note to the Foreign Secretary drew attention to the fact that the traders on the White Nile were to a man slave traders. By exposing the trade, Petherick had led his rivals to make common cause against him, said Colquhoun.[7]

The British Government, however, refused to press Petherick's claim for compensation from the Egyptian Government for the loss of a valuable consignment of ivory. It was not until the end of 1870 that the Foreign Secretary in response to an emotional appeal from the Welshman – 'I am now getting an old man' – agreed to pursue the Egyptians for compensation, but again with the caveat that 'if found to be implicated in the slave trade Mr Petherick would return the money'. Two years later he received £5,151 16s. for the goods and property the Egyptians impounded: equivalent in spending power of £205,000 at 2005 prices.[8] Although Petherick fought long and hard to clear his name, the shadow of slavery cast by Speke and a bunch of 'Khartoum scum' never lifted. When Sir Edward Stanton replaced Colquhoun as Governor-General, Stanton cautioned the home government that 'the trade of the White Nile was in reality so closely connected with the slave trade that it was almost impossible that Mr Petherick's ventures could have been carried on without being mixed up in this traffic.' The British Government never entirely exonerated Petherick.[9]

His dispute with the Royal Geographical Society over whether he complied fully with their agreement to provide succour for Speke and Grant was not resolved satisfactorily either. His bill for £4,172-4s-6d – not far short of £200,000 at 2005 values – for the additional costs of the expedition was never settled and within a few weeks of returning to

England Petherick was humiliated by the announcement that Baker had been awarded the Society's Gold Medal for having, at his own cost, 'fitted out at Khartoum an expedition by which he relieved Speke and Grant'. No mention was made of the Welshman's contribution. Baker was rewarded for opportunism when it was clear he was only authorised to intervene in the event of Petherick's death. 'All I ask is fair play and to be allowed to defend myself,' Petherick protested to Murchison. 'I have returned to England for the purpose of regaining my good name, which during my absence, as you are aware, has grossly suffered from gross misrepresentations. I feel it my duty to protest against a printed statement so prejudicial to my honour and interests.'[10]

The two met the following day at the Museum of Practical Geology in Jermyn Street, London. Nothing was settled. Murchison said that while he wanted to see fair play, the Society, believing the Pethericks were dead, did the honourable thing by employing Baker to provide succour for Speke and Grant. 'It would be very painful for me to act as umpire between Captains Speke and Grant on the one hand, and yourself on the other,' he said. 'But few distant expeditions are conducted without some disagreements among the parties; and I cannot see that in anything which the Royal Geographical Society has done you have cause for complaint.'[11]

The Society had also neglected to mention in its record of *Proceedings* the Pethericks' safe return from Africa. Petherick pressed for a public apology and for some small recognition for Katherine at the very least. The reply from H. W. Bates, Assistant Secretary, on 17 June 1865 exacerbated matters by proposing an agreed statement which in effect blamed Petherick for failing to fulfil his contract because his boats were at Gondokoro for four and a half months from January to mid-May but not until the end of June as agreed. The reason for this, according to the Society, was that Majid, Petherick's agent, was using the boats to transport slaves for which he was eventually clapped in irons. That Speke and Grant did not arrive until almost a year later was disregarded, as was the fact that Petherick continued to station a boat at Gondokoro well after he was contracted to do. The implication in the proposed Memorandum to be entered in the official *Proceedings* of the Society – that the slaves being transported by Majid were from Petherick's own station near Gondokoro – was also damning.

The Society stood its ground, even though in retrospect its complaint against Petherick was wholly irrelevant. A Minute was entered in the record of *Proceedings* (23 June 1865) to the effect that while Petherick was relieved of his responsibility to remain with his boats beyond the end of June 1862, he failed to make provision for the last six weeks of the agreement – when Speke and Grant were still many months away. The Society accepted that there were unavoidable delays due to the early monsoon, but Petherick had failed to discharge his second undertaking to search for the missing explorers. The men sent to search for Speke and Grant were, said the Society, on 'a private trading journey in the direction the travellers were unlikely to be found'. For these reasons the Welshman and his wife were not entitled to any special recognition as he had failed to show that his activities were influenced 'by any other motives than his own private speculations in trade'.[12]

Speke's 'succour dodge' slur stuck, as did the enduring suspicion that Petherick was implicated in the slave trade. His request to appear before the Council was rudely refused although Grant was allowed to present his version of events. 'I protest against this verdict,' wrote Petherick:

> I have been attacked by unfounded statements and worse insinuations when too far away to defend myself; and now prejudice and preconceived opinions have so far prevailed as to induce a committee of gentlemen to deal me this unfair and overpowering blow at a time when, if permitted, I was fully capable of defending myself ... But there is still a higher power – that of public opinion to which I unhesitatingly venture to appeal.[13]

The Pethericks were exhausted; their health permanently damaged. With their funds low, Petherick resubmitted his account for the extra costs incurred, which the Royal Geographical Society was morally obliged to pay, he said. Instead of settling the bill the members were more inclined to pursue him for repayment of the £1,000 in public subscription towards the cost of the expedition. Correspondence with the Foreign Office and the Society continued for several more years, the Welshman desperate for rehabilitation. By 1867 he and Katherine had settled in a house in Henley-on-Thames aptly named *The Tookal* in memory of the grass huts of the Sudan. From there he wrote to the new Foreign Secretary Lord Stanley offering to lead a mission to Abyssinia to negotiate the release of the British Consul Charles Cameron and several other British and German subjects held hostage by the Ethiopian Emperor Tewodros. Petherick's solution was salt, which was as valuable as currency to the Abyssinians. A costly war to release the captives could be avoided by blockading the transit of salt from the coast, he said. This would guarantee the safety of the captives while he negotiated their release. The Foreign Secretary Lord Stanley refused even to meet him, preferring instead to send an expeditionary force from India to free Consul Cameron. Petherick believed that Speke had poisoned the minds of the authorities against him; that his contribution to African exploration was forgotten.

Conclusion

WHAT MIGHT HAVE HAPPENED if Speke had lived and Petherick did get his day in court? The defence in a case of defamation is that the statements complained of are true.

Those who listened to Speke or read his published allegations might easily be tempted to conclude that the Welshman, if not trading in slaves on his own account, was implicated in the traffic in some way; and that Petherick did neglect his duty to provide succour for the explorers at Gondokoro. But on close examination it is clear the slavery charges, at least, were based wholly upon circumstantial evidence which could just as easily point to the contrary: that Petherick was an innocent bystander in the wrong place at the wrong time. If association with slave traders or proximity to trafficking were enough, then Petherick was undoubtedly guilty. In Egypt and the Sudan slavery was rife and it would have been impossible for him to close his eyes entirely, no matter how much a pragmatist. But the jury in a defamation case would have wanted more compelling evidence than innuendo and hearsay emanating from a bunch of Petherick's ruffian rivals. That Speke chose to believe them ahead of the Welshman can be explained either by unscrupulous ambition, or a lack of consideration for the hired help. Speke did regard himself as Petherick's 'commanding officer' while Baker did 'order' Petherick to have boats waiting at Gondokoro on his return from Albert Nyanza. Perhaps nothing more than an unfortunate use of words but part of the problem might have been that the Welshman was always the outsider.[1]

But no crime was committed by Petherick in referring to the slave trader Alphonse de Malzac as a 'friend' even if shocked to discover that in the dungeons beneath the Frenchman's house in Khartoum 100 or more slaves were regularly awaiting transit, chained together in the disease-ridden darkness. In the small European community existing in mid-19th century Sudan one couldn't always choose ones friends. The Governor at El Obeid, Mustafa Pasha, was another 'friend' whose unsavoury reputation Petherick's pragmatism ignored. But did it not make sense to court the friendship of the local potentate under whose tutelage Petherick spent five years harvesting gum arabic in what continues to be one of the remotest and deadliest parts of the world? That the Welshman's partners in the *zariba* at Falaro were the de Bonos – uncle and nephew – was fine if his only interest in the station was as a base for ivory trading. The same cannot be said of Petherick's mysterious partner, the Frenchman M. Grabau for whom there is eye-witness evidence of direct involvement in trafficking slaves along the White Nile. The slaves Petherick (or rather Katherine) discovered on his boats were blamed on a rogue agent engaging in a spot of illicit trade in his employer's absence. For bungling his only attempt to prosecute such offenders – the de Bonos – the Welshman was sternly rebuked by the Consular Judge Sir Edmund Hornby who commented, 'I think it is unfortunate that Mr Consul Petherick is a trader as well as a Consul in that the fact of his being in competition and trading to his own account in competition with the de Bonos in the same trade deprives his evidence, such as it is, of its chief weight.'[2]

By blowing the whistle on the slave trade – with prompting from Katherine – he opened a can of worms which inevitably released a spate of counter accusations that no lone British trader in the Sudan could hope to rebut successfully. Not to be involved in slavery, if only incidentally, required a paragon of moral fortitude which Petherick was not. Almost certainly his domestics were 'slaves', their chores rewarded with bed and board – not unlike the employment conditions familiar to millions in 19th century Europe. His porters carrying ivory to the Nile and his possessions through the equatorial forest would have been in the main slaves hired from native chiefs. Speke, Baker, Stanley – even David Livingstone – all knowingly used slaves as porters, even if, as in the case of Livingstone, as a last resort.

Petherick was a pragmatist in a society where slavery was institutionalised. But that was not good enough for a British public that regarded slavery in the Sudan as identical to that in North America when, in fact, it was different. Generally, the plantation slaves of the Americas suffered greater hardship than the chattel slaves of Islam and native African tribes. Until 1859 Petherick successfully sidestepped the issue, but as British Consul with a new wife whose eyes were wide open, he was unable to reconcile the dilemma between his pragmatism, and official and moral pressure to expose the dark secrets of the White Nile traders. Failure to do so wrecked his reputation.

The Welshman's case was not helped by appearing at times as an apologist for his former employer, the Viceroy Mohammad Ali Pasha under whose stewardship slavery flourished. Petherick's suggestion that the trade had only raised its ugly head during his absence in England was too much like an excuse for failing to take decisive action in the past. The big difference, post-1859, was that Katherine was instrumental in redefining his attitude. It was she who discovered the slaves aboard his boats, who repeatedly drew attention to the activities of the slave traders along the river, whose heart ached for the children herded like cattle across the desert by Arab slavers and for the old slave who dragged himself to the river to die. Would Petherick have noticed? After all, no sooner had they taken possession of the Consulate in Khartoum and he gave Katherine a 12-year-old child slave to train as a seamstress.

The use of slaves as domestic servants was commonplace throughout the Arab and African world. In fact, it still was a hundred years later according to relatives of mine who lived in Alexandria in 1956 during the dictatorship of Colonel Gamal Abdel Nasser. One of Nasser's colonels living around the corner from their apartment 'bought' an eight-year-old child from her parents for a handful of Egyptian Pounds. The child was trained as a domestic in return for bed and board until one day after being sent to the local shop she ran off with the money, never to be seen again.

But did Petherick's interest in slaves extend beyond using them as domestics? Abolition by Britain and the United States had not entirely disposed of the view that the white man had a God-given right to exploit Black Africans. Coincidentally, such sentiments were echoed in a letter to the *Times* by the secretary of the Royal Geographical Society, Francis Galton who sparred with the Welshman in the dispute over succour for Speke and Grant. After taking issue with those who thought the African 'our equal in brain and heart', Galton continued:

I do not think that the average Negro cares for his liberty as much as an Englishman, or even as a serf-born Russian; and I do believe that if we can, in any fair way, possess ourselves of his services, we have an equal right to utilize them to our advantage as the State has to drill and coerce a recruit who in a moment of intoxication has accepted the Queen's shilling, or as a shopkeeper to order about a boy whose parents had bound him over to an apprenticeship ... these people are treated as children by their masters and compelled to do what they dislike for their future good and for that of the society at large.

> Therefore, I say with regard to these Negroes, if we can by any legitimate, or even *quasi*-legitimate means possess ourselves to a right to their services, and if we can insure that our mastership will elevate them, and not degrade them, then by all means work them well ...[3]

Galton disagreed, however, with the more extremist view prevailing in some quarters of Victorian society that because Africans were always fighting among themselves and selling their prisoners into slavery why should the white man abstain from buying?

If the Welshman did cross the line it was never once mentioned outside the White Nile trading community until the Austrian Vice-Consul Natterer gave currency to the allegations in a report to his government. Petherick's rivals thirsting for revenge after his botched arrests conspired against him, and a British Foreign Office influenced by Speke refused Petherick a hearing. Natterer did back off, pleading a misunderstanding before he died. As for the evidence of Arab witnesses to Petherick's alleged indiscretions, that simply disappeared. One of the few surviving official documents relating to slave traffic on the White Nile at this time is in the Egyptian Government archives held at the library in Alexandria. Dated 1851, the document is a complaint from the then Foreign Minister Istifān Bey that European traders – no specific mention of Petherick – were 'travelling through the countryside with their slaves and armed servants committing offences against the people', evading tax and obstructing the administration.[4]

By sacking Petherick, the Foreign Office publicly endorsed these accusations, while stiffening the resolve of the Royal Geographical Society to take issue. If Petherick had no skeletons in his backpack, would the Society have quibbled about the wholly academic point that for barely four weeks – when Speke and Grant were many months away – there was no boat waiting at Gondokoro? If Baker had not intervened opportunistically, the Welshman would have been applauded by Speke, Grant, and the Society for having boats and men awaiting the eventual arrival of the missing explorers no matter how long it took. John Petherick was cast out by Baker's opportunism and Speke's ambition. Ironically, by sacking him without a trial and closing the Consulate in Khartoum, the Foreign Office demonstrated a practical disregard for suppressing slavery in Central Africa.

In the opinion of Katherine, Petherick was an honourable and caring individual. Is it possible that this intelligent, perceptive woman was duped by a tough White Nile trader intent on carrying her off to Africa as a slave trader's wife? As it happened, she was his greatest advocate: her husband a victim of malicious rumour; never cruel or indifferent to others; a man of rare self-control and high moral principles. From the moment Katherine stepped ashore in Egypt, Petherick raised his head above the parapet to champion emancipation, albeit clumsily but at considerable personal risk.

Nevertheless, he honestly doubted whether abolition was at all possible while slavery prevailed within Islam. Perhaps characteristically, the solution advocated by the White Nile trader was the eradication of Islamism. 'Its [slavery] entire abolition, everyone with knowledge of the domestic habits of Musselmans will agree, is next to impossible,' he said. 'Nothing less than the subversion of their religion, the suppression of polygamy and its consequent usages, will [prevent] slavery which, to every Mahommedan, is a domestic necessity. If the French and English Governments were to combine and put the screw on the Egyptian Government ... the trade [might] speedily be limited [and] by gradually curtailing these limits, slaves will become too great a luxury for any but the wealthy to indulge in. Thus, by introducing the thin end of the wedge, a change of domestic habits may, in course of time, be realized.'[5]

As for his legacy, there are no memorials to mark his passage; no mountain, lake or town commemorating Petherick; and nor is he remembered as a civilizing influence unlike the missionary-explorer Livingstone. Petherick was the trader-explorer whose geographical achievements were incidental to profiting from the wilderness. If the main concerns of mid-19th century Victorian interest in Africa were botanical observations, geology and geographical surveys, Petherick did that as well. He explored the Nile's two longest tributaries, Bahr al-Ghazal (445m; 716k) and the Sobat (220m; 354k); the Jur River (301m; 485k), a tributary of the Bahr al-Ghazal; and the Lol River emptying into the swamplands of the Sudd. Petherick covered immense distances during seventeen years in Egypt, the Sudan and Central Africa. Even the Royal Geographical Society, which has given Petherick little credit for his achievements, on one occasion relented by publishing in its *Journal*, albeit briefly, an extract and map from a paper delivered in 1865 entitled 'Land Journey Westward of the White Nile,' giving measurements of the Nile tributaries south of the Sobat River to within 4°46 N. Latitude of the equator. In the view of one the most distinguished cartographers of the 19th century, the German Dr August Petermann, editor of the prestigious *Mittheilungen aus Justus Perthes Geographischer Anstalt über wichtige neue Erforschungen auf dem Gesamtgebiet der Geographie*, Petherick's map was a significant contribution to African exploration. Of the Welshman's journey, Peterman said, 'We must acknowledge it to be the most important journey of all hitherto accomplished in the territory between the Upper White Nile and the Djour.'[6]

Sadly, the controversy with Speke not only obscured Petherick's geographical achievements, but also his considerable additions to natural history. Both he and Katherine were accomplished artists, his sketchbook in the Wellcome Library testifying to a more discerning individual than that portrayed by his critics. A talent for crafting neat line-drawings of native weapons, domestic utensils, animals and plants would not usually be associated with White Nile traders. By comparison, Speke's artistic contributions were primitive and childlike.[7]

Petherick was also an avid collector of skins, animal skulls, and even human ones; on one occasion asking Dr Murie to boil the heads of two natives severed in battle and after removing the brains send them to the Royal Society of Surgeons for study. An extensive collection of fish caught by Petherick in the Lower and Upper Nile provided the British Museum with the world's most complete series of fishes of the Nile.[8]

He sent a baby hippopotamus and a pair of Balaeniceps Rex (the shoebill) – a large stork-like bird from the Sudd with a massive shoe-shaped bill – to England. For some unexplained reason, the baby hippo and its native keeper ended up in a circus in the United States while the birds were probably among a large number of live specimens lost when the boat transporting them downriver to Alexandria capsized in attempting to cross a cataract. Among the collection of animal heads Petherick deposited in the British Museum were those of a male and female antelope from the wetlands identified by the curator Dr J. E. Gray as a new species *Kobus mari* (Mrs Gray's Nile Lechwe). Petherick provided the museum with two other new species from Central Africa – a freshwater turtle and a chamaeleon. A genus of plant was also named after the Pethericks who were enthusiastic botanists.[9]

Of Petherick's large collection of native artefacts many were lost when another boat sank. But at least 142 survived to reach England to form part of the founding collection of world anthropological and archaeological exhibits at the Pitt Rivers Museum at the University of Oxford. The museum was established in 1874 when General Augustus Pitt Rivers donated his private collection of 20,000 items. Petherick's collection of native arms, and items of husbandry, hunting, costume and domestic use procured from 1853–8 on his White Nile and Bahr al-Ghazal expeditions, were bought by General Pitt Rivers at auction in London in June 1862. These items must have been sold on Petherick's instructions since he and Katherine were en route to Egypt at the time. Some of the Petherick exhibits displayed at the Pitt Rivers Museum are irreplaceable – biographical pointers to native African tribes and customs that are no longer found in Central Africa. Petherick's varied ethnological interests even extended to the compilation of a crude vocabulary of native language.[10]

Katherine Petherick knew her husband's weaknesses, his quick temper and heavy hand. But still, for her, he was the knight errant roaming through the savage wilderness; strong and terrible when necessary without being brutal; subduing natives with a mixture of audacity and prudence, without sentimentalism, or maudlin philanthropy.[11] If Petherick had once been the unfettered adventurer who dared not admit his past, he reinvented himself under Katherine's restraining influence.

On the balance of the circumstantial evidence it would be astonishing if Petherick the pragmatist did not have something to hide: that he at least dabbled in slavery, maybe not on his own account but indirectly by permitting his boats to be used to traffic slaves in lieu of paying his mercenaries. But there's not a scrap of credible evidence to put before a jury. No one will ever know for sure: slave traders didn't give receipts! Yet Katherine was too discerning to have been fooled, her enduring respect and affection for the Welsh adventurer the surest sign he was but a sad victim of the bitter rivalry over the source of the Nile. At the very least, like other White Nile traders he was guilty of ignoring the catastrophic consequences their aggressive demands were having upon the indigenous people. Petherick, whether he knew it or not, conspired – with Speke, Baker, Burton and others – to divide and rule, the imperative characterizing the end of the classic period of exploration and laying the foundation for the colonial scramble for Africa.

He died from bronchial pneumonia in lodgings at 54 Lancaster Road in Kensington on 15 July 1882, aged 69, by which time what remained of his valuable collection of native artefacts had been sold to fend off bankruptcy. Even then, the Royal Geographical Society refused to relent, publishing an obituary worded as if to hide the real tragedy behind the search for the source of the Nile. Although grudgingly, the Society admitted Petherick's contribution to exploration in Central Africa, it drew a veil over events that culminated in a quarrel at least equal to the one between Speke and Burton:

> ... [Petherick] was for some years prior to the great expedition of Speke and Grant engaged as a trader in the Egyptian Sudan and in the course of his operations penetrated to the south in the regions west of the Nile further than had been reached by any previous traveller ... Having been appointed British Consul in the Sudan, the Royal Geographical Society availed themselves of an offer by him to meet Captains Speke and Grant at Gondokoro ... Petherick who with his heroic wife had made a long detour west of the White Nile

and met with endless obstacles and disappointments was not there to meet them. The promised boats and provisions were there but Captain Speke being disappointed with Petherick's proceedings preferred to accept the proffered help of Sir Samuel Baker ... The result was disastrous for Petherick. Soon after Captain Speke's arrival in England, Petherick was deprived of the consulship at Khartoum, and because of some difficulties arising at the same time with native officials, his mercantile affairs fell into disorder, threatening him with ruin, which was only averted by the Egyptian Government making him some compensation for his losses. His later years were spent in retirement in the West Country.[12]

Katherine had died five years earlier, aged 48, at St Goran in Cornwall in March 1877. Despite her enduring faith and support, the Welshman never erased the stain that denied him a place in the pantheon dedicated to African exploration.

Notes

Chapter 1

1. Wilkins, Charles, *The History of the Iron, Steel, Tinplate and Other Trades of Wales* (1903), p 303; Kenrick, G. S., Varteg Ironworks, lecture, Pontypool Mechanics Institute 1840, Chartist Archives, Newport Public Library.
2. Commissioners of Inquiry into the state of education in Wales, Part 11, Brecknock, Cardigan, Radnor and Monmouth, 1847, Law Library, Cardiff University, pp. 290–1; Kenrick, G. S., lecture,1840, Chartist Archives, Newport Public Library.
3. James, Charles Herbert James, *What I remember about myself and old Merthyr* (1889).
4. Wilkins, p. 303–4.
5. TNA, HO 52/16, deposition, John Petherick Senior, 20 June 1831 at second inquest on John Hughes.
6. Ibid.
7. Ibid.
8. Ibid.
9. *John Petherick, watercolours from a family scrap-album*, exhibition, Stephen Somerville and Anthony Reed, Bernheimers, George Street, London, catalogue, Merthyr Public Library.
10. Author's note: Darwin later attributed his geological knowledge to Sedgwick's mentoring although the Cambridge professor and Church of English clergyman vigorously rejected his evolutionary theories. Nevertheless, they remained good friends.
11. Geikie, Archibald, *Life of Sir Roderick I. Murchison, based on his journals and letters* (London: John Murray, 1875), letter from Murchison to his wife, 8 October 1839, pp. 282–3.

Chapter 2

1. Drescher, Seymour, *Abolition: A history of slavery and anti-slavery*, 2009, pp. 4–5.
2. Senior, N. W., *Conversations and Journals in Egypt and Malta* (London: 1882), p. 207.
3. Gray, R., *A History of the Southern Sudan, 1839–1889* (London: 1861), pp. 66–9; TNA, F.O. 84/1120 'Memorandum by Mr Petherick', December 1860; TNA, F.O. 84/1260 Stanton to Claredon, Alexandria, 9 May 1866; F.O. 141/121 Borg to Vivian, Cairo, 23 August 1878.
4. TNA, FO 84/1304, 1305, 1354, 1371; TNA, FO 84/1120; FO 141/57, Petherick to Colquhoun, Cairo, 17 March 1865.
5. Petherick, John, *Egypt, the Soudan and Central Africa* (William Blackwood and Sons, Edinburgh: 1861), pp. 2–6
6. Ibid., p. 7.
7. Ibid., pp. 7–8
8. Ibid., pp. 9–10.
9. Ibid., pp. 10–11.
10. Burckhardt, John Lewis, *Travels in Syria and the Holy Land* (1822).
11. Black, Matthew, and Robert Davidson, *Constantin von Tischendorf and the Greek New Testament* (Glasgow: University of Glasgow Press, 1981).
12. Petherick, *Egypt, the Soudan and Central Africa*, p. 42.
13. Ibid., p. 44.
14. Ibid., pp. 83–5.

Chapter 3

1. Spaulding, Jay, 'Slavery, Land Tenure and Social Class in the Northern Turkish Sudan 1820–1881', *International Journal of African Historical Studies 15*, 1 (1982), pp. 1–20; Pallme, Ignatius, *Travels in Kordofan* (J. Madden and Co., London: 1844), pp. 108–109; pp. 213–14.
2. Petherick, John, *Egypt, the Soudan and Central Africa: with explorations from Khartoum on the White Nile to the Regions of the Equator* (London: Tinsley, 1859), pp. 301, 307.
3. Petherick, *Egypt, the Soudan and Central Africa*, p. 336.
4. Ibid., p. 128.
5. Pallme, *Travels in Kordofan*, p. 306.
6. Ibid., pp. 110–12, 270–2, 294, 320–4.
7. Holroyd, Richard, 'Notes on a Journey to Kordofan in 1836–37', *Journal of the Royal Geographical Society*, vol. IX, Part 2, February 1839, p. 177.
8. Cumming, Duncan, *The Gentleman Savage* (London: Century Hutchinson, 1987), p. 134.
9. Petherick, *Travels*, pp. 320–1.

10. D'Eichthal, Gustave, and Urbain, Ismayl, *Lettres sur la race noir, et la race blanche* (Paris: 1849).

11. Palme, *Travels in Kordofan*, p. 59; Ruppell, Eduard, *Reizen in Nubien Kordofan und dem Petraischen Arabien Vorzuglich in Geograpghisch Statistischen Hinsicht*, Frankfurt am Main, 1829, pp. 39–40; Reclus, Élisée, *Africa and its Inhabitants*, ed. A. H. Keane, vol. III, pp. 25–7 (London: Virtue).

12. *Times*, 27 January 1859, p. 6.

13. Petherick, *Egypt, the Soudan and Central Africa*, p. 116.

14. TNA, F.O. 78/840, Murray to Viscount Palmerston, 5 June 1850; TNA, FO 78/2253, 24 October 1850, Palmerston confirmation of Petherick's retrospective appointment.

15. Spaulding, Jay, 'Slavery, Land Tenure and Social Class in the Northern Turkish Sudan 1820–1881', *International Journal of African Historical Studies 15*, 1 (1982), pp. 1–20; Petherick, *Egypt, the Soudan and Central Africa*, pp. 311–12.

16. MacMichael, H. A., *The Tribes of Northern and Central Kurdistan* (Cambridge University Press, 1912); Schweinfurth, G., *The Heart of Africa*, maps, 'Tribes of Southern Sudan' and 'Principal zaribas of the Bahr al-Ghazal'.

17. Petherick, John, *Egypt, the Soudan and Central Africa: with explorations from Khartoum on the White Nile to the Regions of the Equator* (London: Tinsley, 1859), p. 312.

18. Ibid., p. 330.

Chapter 4

1. Baker, Samuel, *The Albert N'yanza, Great Basin of the Nile* (The Echo Library, 2005).

2. Ibid., pp. 22–5.

3. Petherick, John, *Egypt, the Sudan and Central Africa* (London: Tinsley, 1859), p. 345.

4. Beachey, R. W., *The East African Ivory Trade in the Nineteenth Century* (Cambridge University Press), pp. 279–80.

5. Sforza, G., ed., *Un Lucchese in Africa, lettree di Adolfo Antognoli* (Lucca: 1878). Author's note: The 'dollars' referred to by Antognoli could have been either the 'Maria Theresa Dollar', the silver bullion 'thaler' circulating in eastern or northern Africa at this time as an investment rather than for use in day-to-day commerce; or the 'Spanish Dollar', a silver coin which by the late 18th century was an international currency, corresponding in size to the 'thaler'. In English, 'dollar' was used to refer to all such coins. It is impossible to be sure what Lucca was referring to.

6. Petherick, John, *Egypt, The Sudan and Central Africa* (London: Tinsley, 1859), pp. 262–69, pp. 379–86.
7. Udal, John, 'Sudan Studies', No 17, September 1995, pp. 2–21; Beachey, R. W., '*The East African Ivory Trade in the Nineteenth Century*' (Cambridge University Press), pp. 279–80.
8. Schirmer, H., 'Les Traites de Partage de 1894 en Afrique Centrale', *Annales de Géographe*, vol. 5, Numéro 20 (1896), pp. 202–15.
9. Count Gleichen, Captain, *Handbook: The Sudan* (London: 1898), p. 213.

Chapter 5

1. Udal, *Sudan Studies* (1995), pp. 2–22.
2. Petherick, *Egypt, the Sudan and Central Africa* (London: Tinsley, 1859), p. 345.
3. Ibid., pp. 349–50.
4. Ibid., pp. 362–69.
5. Ibid., pp. 379–82.
6. Petherick, John and Katherine, *Travels in Central Africa* (London: Tinsley, 1869), Volume 1, p. 337.
7. Ibid., pp. 385–86.
8. TNA, FO, 78/1542, Petherick to Consul-General, 13 August 1860; HHSA, Alexandrien, X11/1874/9462/0, Letter G. Filek, Chancellor to the Consulate General, to Count Rechberg-Rothenlowen, Minister of Foreign Affairs, 19 July 1864.
9. Carnochan, W. B., *The Sad Story of Burton, Speke, and The Nile; or, was John Hanning Speke a Cad?* (Stanford: Stanford University Press, 2006), pp 85–6; Maitland, Alexander, *Speke and the Discovery of the Source of the Nile* (London: Constable, 1871), p 181; Petherick, pp. 2, 125; 2, 125–6; 2, 143; 2, 140.
10. Carnochan, W. B., *The Sad Story*, p. 87.
11. Petherick, *Egypt, the Sudan and Central Africa*, pp. 397–400.
12. Ibid., pp. 403–6.
13. Udal, 'Sudan Studies'; Santi and Hill, *The Europeans in the Sudan, 1834–1878*.
14. Petherick, *Egypt, the Sudan and Central Africa*, pp. 307–10, 403–6.
15. Fabian, Johannes, *Out of our minds, Reason and Madness in the Exploration of Central Africa* (Berkeley: University of California Press, 2000), pp. 78–86.
16. Santi, P., and Hill, R., *The Europeans in the Sudan, 1834–1878* (Oxford: 1980), p. 22.
17. Wauvermans, H., ed., 'Pruyssenaere, letters to his parents and others', *Bull. Soc. Roy. Géogr. D'Anvers*, xix (1930), p. 289.
18. Petherick, *Egypt, the Sudan and Central Africa*, p. 437.
19. Ibid. p. 398.

Chapter 6

1. Speke, John Hanning, 'What Led to the Discovery of the Source of the Nile' (Edinburgh and London: William Blackwood and Sons, 1864), pp. 305–19.

2. Moorehead, Alan, The White Nile (London: Hamish Hamilton, 1960), p. 24.

3. Speke, Journal of the Discovery of the Source of the Nile, 1863, pp. 209, 231; Petherick, Travels in Central Africa, p.16; letter from Grant to John Blackwood, no date, 1863, National Library of Scotland. MS. 4181; Speke, original MS. Draft of the Journal, pp. 319, 320, NLS, MS. 4872, Blackwood Collection.

4. TNA, FO 78/1465.

5. TNA, FO 78/1542, Petherick to Consul-General Colquhoun, 13 August 1860.

6. Santi, P., and Hill, R., The Europeans in the Sudan 1834–1878 (Oxford: Clarendon Press: 1980), pp. 177–80, Note 25. Author's note: The map entitled 'Sketch map of John Petherick's travels in the years 1853–1858' appears in his book, Egypt, the Soudan and Central Africa with explorations from Khartoum to the White Nile to the Equator (1861). According to Santi and Hill, Petherick's claim to have reached the equator is 'pure pseudo-travel' though he may have been the first European to record the existence of one of the small, shallow lakes south of Bahr al-Ghazal.

7. Royal Geographical Society, Proceedings, 26 May 1862, p. 175.

8. TNA, FO 78/1542, Petherick to Russell.

9. TNA, FO 78/1612.

10. Jordans weekend reference.

11. House of Commons Select Committee on Income Tax, 1861, 8:1 p. 339; Farr, William, 'Statistics of the Civil Service of England with observations on the constitution of funds to provide for fatherless children and widows', Journal of the Royal Statistical Society of London, 12 (1849) pp. 134–5; Yeo, Eileen Yeo, and Thompson, E. P., eds, The Unknown Mayhew (London: 1971), pp. 157–8.

12. Petherick, John and Katherine, Travels in Central Africa and Exploration of Western Nile Tributaries, Appendix A (London: Tinsley, 1869), Speke to Petherick, 25 September 1859, p. 78; ibid., Speke to Petherick, October 1859, p. 79; Petherick, John and Katherine, Travels in Central Africa, Appendix A, pp. 80–1.

13. Petherick, Travels in Central Africa, Appendix A, pp. 80–1, letter Speke to Shaw, 2 January 1860.

14. Royal Geographical Society, Proceedings, vol. xii, p. 20, 12 November 1860; ibid., xx, p. 89.

Chapter 7

1. Petherick, John and Katherine, *Travels in Central Africa*, pp. 2–5.
2. Grant, J. A., *A Walk across Africa* (1864), p. 402.
3. Santi, P., and Hill, R., *The Europeans in the Sudan,* p. 178, note 23.
4. Petherick, John and Katherine, *Travels in Central Africa*, p. 16.
5. Ibid., pp. 45–7.
6. Ibid., p. 28.
7. Ibid., p. 32.
8. Ibid., pp. 35–6.
9. Ibid., pp. 37, 45.
10. Ibid., p. 57.
11. Ibid., p. 62.
12. Ibid., p. 66.
13. Ibid., p. 70.
14. Ibid., p. 71.
15. Ibid., p. 73.
16. Ibid., p. 81.

Chapter 8

1. Baker, Samuel, *The Albert N'yanza* (The Echo Library, 2005), p. 26.
2. Hall, Richard, *Lovers on the Nile* (London: Collins, 1980), p. 15.
3. Hall, *Lovers*, p.14.
4. Baker, *The Albert N'yanza*, p. 16.
5. Ibid.
6. Hall, *Lovers*, pp. 72–3.
7. Ibid., pp. 89–90.
8. Ibid., p. 95.
9. Ibid., p. 97.
10. Ibid., pp. 104–5.
11. Ibid., pp. 134–5; TNA, FO 141/48, Petherick to Colquhoun, 24 May 1862, from Nouau on the White Nile.
12. TNA, FO 141/48, Petherick to Colquhoun, 24 May 1862, from Nouau on the White Nile.
13. TNA, FO, 84/1181, 17 June 1862, translation provided by Amabile de Bono.
14. Ibid.
15. Ibid.
16. Petherick, John and Katherine, *Travels in Central Africa*, pp. 136–7.
17. Author's note: Holland and Holland, London, was founded in 1835 and became the Royal Gunmaker in 1885.

18. Petherick, John and Katherine, *Travels in Central Africa*, p. 175.

19. Ibid., p. 195.

20. Ibid., p. 231.

21. Ibid., p. 207.

22. Petherick, J, 'Land Journey Westward of the White Nile, from Abu Kuka to Gondokoro', *Proceedings* (The Royal Geographical Society), p. 296, read to the Society 25 April 1864.

23. Petherick, John and Katherine, *Travels in Central Africa*, p. 229.

24. Ibid., pp. 274–99.

Chapter 9

1. Petherick, John and Katherine, *Travels in Central Africa* (London: Tinsley, 1869), Volume I, p. 300.

2. Ibid., pp. 205–7.

3. Ibid., pp. 306–7; The Royal Geographical Society, *Proceedings*, Khartoum, 24 November 1862, vol. vii, p. 78.

4. Catania, Charles, *Andrea de Bono, Maltese Explorer on the White Nile* (Minerva Press, 2001), pp. 277–8; Maitland, Alexander, *Speke and the Discovery of the Source of the Nile* (London: Constable, 1971), p.172.

5. Santi, Paul (translated by Richard Hill), *The Europeans in the Sudan 1834–1878* (Oxford: Clarendon Press, 1980), pp. 124–5.

6. Petherick, John and Katherine, *Travels in Central Africa* (London: Tinsley, 1869), vol. 1, p. 337.

7. Royal Geographical Society, *Proceedings*, vol. vii, no. 5.

8. Baker, Samuel, *The Albert N'yanza, Great Basin of the Nile and Explorations of the Nile Sources* (London: 1866), p.50.

9. Baker, *The Albert N'Yanza*, pp. 52, 53, 56; *Times*, report of the 'Proceedings,' Royal Geographical Society, 24 June 1863, page 7, col. F; *Times*, 'Proceedings,' RGS, 11 February 1863; John Hanning Speke, *Journal of the Discovery of the Source of the Nile* (London: Blackwood, 1863), p. 601.

10. Speke, *Journal of the Discovery of the Source of the Nile* (London: Blackwood, 1863), p. 177 Speke.

11. Letter, Speke to Blackwood, 18 April 1860, postscript, National Library of Scotland, L. S., MS. 4154.

12. Grant, James Augustus, *A Walk Across Africa* (London: 1864), p. 366.

13. Letter from Mrs Petherick to Mona McQuie from Khartoum, 2 October 1863, *Travels in Central Africa* (London: Tinsley, 1869), vol. II, p. 19.

14. Petherick, John and Katherine, *Travels in Central Africa*, p. 387.

15. Ibid., Appendix A, pp. 128–30.

16. Ibid., letter, Katherine Petherick to sister, 2 October 1863.

17. Petherick, John and Katherine, *Travels in Central Africa*, Appendix A, p. 133.

18. Petherick, John and Katherine, *Travels in Central Africa*, Appendix A, letter, Lord Russell to Petherick, 31 October 1863, p. 152; *The Athenaeum*, letter from Eugène de Pruyssenaere, 9 April 1864; Hall, Richard, *Lovers on the Nile* (Collins: London, 1980), p. 127.

19. Letter, James Murie to Peter McQuie, Gondokoro, 19 March 1863, *Travels in Central Africa*, pp. 314–15.

20. Ibid., 314.

21. Petherick, John and Katherine, *Travels in Central Africa*, p. 318.

22. Ibid., p. 322.

23. Ibid., p. 326.

24. Petherick, John and Katherine, *Travels in Central Africa*, vol. II, letter to sister, pp. 22, 30.

25. Ibid., p. 64.

26. Ibid., pp. 22, 25.

27. Ibid., p. 35.

28. Petherick, John and Katherine, *Travels in Central Africa*, vol. I, pp. 365–9.

29. Ibid., p. 25, vol. II, letter, Katherine Petherick to sister, 12 May 1864.

30. Baker, *The Albert N'yanza, Great Basin of the Nile and Explorations of the Nile Sources* (London: 1896), p. 192.

31. Petherick, John and Katherine, *Travels in Central Africa*, vol. II, pp. 31–2.

32. Ibid., p. 59.

Chapter 10

1. Royal Geographical Society, *Proceedings*, vol. viii, no. III, p. 19; RGS, *Proceedings*, 'Annual Address', May 25, 1863, vol. viii, no. IV.

2. Burton, Richard Francis, *The Nile Basin, Part 1, Showing Tanganyika to be Ptolemy's Western lake reservoir* (London: Tinsley, 1864), a memoir read to the Royal Geographical Society, 14 November 1864, p. 68.

3. Ibid., pp. 71–2

4. Ibid.

5. *The Athenaeum*, 29 August 1863.

6. 'The Death of Speke,' *Blackwood's Edinburgh Magazine*, October 1864, pp. 514–16.

7. *Westminster Review*, no. 50, April 1865, p. 315.

8. Burton, *The Nile Basin*, p. 28.

9. Isabel, Lady Burton, *The Life of Sir Richard Burton*, vol. 2, p. 426.

10. Ibid.

11. Maitland, Alexander, *Speke* (London: Constable, 1971), pp. 214–16.

12. Brodie, Fawn M., *The Devil Drives* (New York: 1967), p. 226; Farwell, Byron, *Burton* (London: 1963), p. 241.

13. Brodie, *The Devil Drives*, pp. 220–30
14. Burton, *The Nile Basin*, 'Prefatory Remarks', pp. 3–4.

Chapter 11

1. Petherick, John and Katherine, *Travels in Central Africa*, from Mrs Petherick's Notebook, vol. II, pp. 66–7, letter to sister, Mona McQuie, November 1864.
2. Ibid., 'Mrs Petherick's Notebook', p. 68.
3. *Times*, letter from P. B. McQuie, 24 December 1863, p. 6, col. F.
4. *Times*, letter from Speke, 28 December 1863, p. 9, col. D.
5. *Times*, letter (posthumous), Speke, 3 May 1864, p. 7, col. F.
6. *Times*, letter from John Tinné, 5 October 1864, p. 12, col. C.
7. TNA, FO, 78/2253, Colquhoun to Earl Russell, 6 April 1865.
8. TNA, FO, 78/2253, Petherick to Earl Stanton.
9. TNA, FO, 78/2253, Stanton to the Earl of Clarendon, 14 January 1870.
10. *Travels*, Appendix A, pp. 161–4.
11. Ibid., pp. 161–4
12. Ibid., pp. 169–72.
13. Ibid., pp. 173–4.

Conclusion

1. Santi and Hill (eds), *The Europeans in the Sudan 1834–1878*, p. 182.
2. TNA, FO, 84/1181, Hornby to Lord Russell.
3. *Times*, letter, 26 December 1857, p. 10.
4. Archives de Ministère des Affaires Étrangères, Paris, Correspondance Commerciale, Alexandrie, 34 Fos 81–3, Istifān Bey to the French Consul-General Le Moyne, 29 September 1851; Santi and Hill, eds, *The Europeans in the Sudan 1834–1878*, p. 177.
5. Petherick, John and Katherine, *Travels in Central Africa*, pp. 158–9.
6. Ibid., Appendix A, p. 184.
7. MS. 5787–5789, Wellcome Library, Euston Road, London.
8. Petherick, John and Katherine, *Travels in Central Africa*, Appendix C, p. 194.
9. Ibid., pp. 474–5; Appendix B, p. 189.
10. Pitt Rivers Museum, Oxford, 1874 Catalogue, pl. IV, no. 39 [RTS 13/5/2005]; also J. G. Wood, 1868, *The Natural History of Man*, p. 525; J. Petherick, 1861, 'On the arms of the Arab and Negro tribes of Central Africa, bordering on the White Nile', *Journal of the Royal United Service Institution*, IV, no. 13, p. 176, no. 15.
11. 'Life in Central Africa', *Blackwood's Magazine*, 1860, pp. 440–53.
12. Royal Geographical Society, *Proceedings*, October–November 1882, p. 700.

Appendices

MORE ABOUT THE MAIN PLAYERS

Alexine Tinné

The daughter of one of the wealthiest families in the Netherlands, she was educated in the best European fashion, spent her holidays in London and Paris, and spoke fluent French and English. For a time the Tinnés settled in England and although returning to the Netherlands Alexine's stepbrother remained in Liverpool and was a friend and neighbour of Katherine Petherick's brother-in-law, the accountant Peter McQuie.

A fine horsewoman and linguist, Alexine's combination of wealth and beauty was irresistible, reputedly, leading to a broken romance. But after a visit to the pyramids when nineteen, she fell in love with Egypt, travelling by camel to the Red Sea with her mother, visiting the Holy Land and Damascus at a time when it was unsafe for European women in those parts.

Following the disaster on the Nile, Alexine spent five years living on an island in the Nile until deciding to become the first European woman to cross the Sahara. In 1869, after recruiting two Dutch sailors, the expedition headed from Algeria to Lake Chad, the goal of her earlier expedition with her mother. The French explorer Duveyrier, one of the few Europeans to explore the Sahara had two years previously spent some time amongst the Tuareg. Alexine's plan was to follow his route to Lake Chad, then return through Darfur to the Nile and Khartoum. To attempt such a journey was the African equivalent of Scott's expedition to the South Pole fifty years later! This would also prove fatal.

The first stage was without mishap, apart from the usual sandstorms. It was when the caravan was being escorted to a rendezvous with a Tuareg chieftain that disaster struck. Knowing the hazards of desert travel, Alexine had taken along not only an ice-making machine as a gift for the Sheikh but also two iron tanks of water carried by camels. But rumours spread that the tanks were filled with gold coins, not water, and as they left an oasis they were surrounded by Tuareg warriors and an altercation occurred between Alexine's Arab servants and the newcomers. One of the Dutch sailors tried to break up the fight but was speared, the Tuareg then turning on Alexine, and cutting off her hand as she drew a revolver. The second Dutchman was killed trying to defend her, their attackers riding off, leaving Alexine to bleed to death in the sand.

Alexine and her mother were extraordinary in an era when the very last thing expected of Victorian women was that they would trot off to darkest Africa. Dilettantes maybe, but they did return from their adventures with valuable new animal and plant material, including a set of botanical drawings *Plantae Tinneanae*. But apart from this little is known about Alexine. Harriet kept a diary but it is incomplete. Alexine wrote many letters, but these and her crates of ethnological specimens stored in London were destroyed during the blitz in the Second World War. A small obelisk was erected by David Livingstone on the banks of the White Nile near Juba in the Republic of South Sudan, marking the furthest point reached by Alexine of whom Livingstone said:

> The work of Speke and Grant is deserving of highest commendation, inasmuch as they opened up an immense tract of previously unexplored country. But none rises higher in my estimation than the Dutch lady, Miss Tinne, who after the severest domestic afflictions, nobly persevered in the teeth of every difficulty.

James Augustus Grant

Grant was the fourth and youngest son of James Grant, a clergyman at Nairn. He bought a commission in the 8th native Bengal infantry in 1846, his acquaintance with John Hanning Speke dating from this time. They served together, were much the same age, and both devoted to field sports, especially the hunting of big game. When Speke was commissioned by the Royal Geographical Society to return to Africa to locate the point at which he believed the Nile exited Victoria Nyanza, Grant's offer to join him was immediately accepted. The conduct of the expedition was under the direction of Speke, and on all occasions Grant proved himself a loyal and devoted follower, not a shade of jealousy or distrust or even ill temper ever coming between them on their journey, he wrote later.

Grant was six feet two inches in height, broad, and had great strength and endurance. Baker described him as 'one of the most loyal, charming characters in the world, perfectly unselfish, and always ready to give to his companion in travel, all the honour for the expedition'. But due to illness Grant never saw the point at which the Nile poured out of Victoria Nyanza.

Sir Francis Richard Burton

Burton claimed descent from Louis XIV, although his more immediate family were prosperous country folk from Westmoreland and his mother a wealthy heiress. After an early education delivered by private tutors, he went to Trinity College, Oxford but hating every moment was finally expelled for attending a steeplechase against college rules. As a parting shot, 'Ruffian Jack' – as he was known to brother officers in the army of the East India Company – drove his horse and carriage over the college flower beds! Burton's outrageous behaviour, in particular his lifelong interest in the sexual practices of the indigenous peoples of Africa and Asia, set him apart, it being widely assumed that he had experienced the activities vividly described in his journals. The erudite and popular author of *Lake Regions of Central Africa*, one of the most esteemed exploration journals ever written, his unorthodox investigations led him into brothels disguised in eastern garb and to places others dared not go.

Sir Samuel White Baker, and Florence, Lady Baker

Baker was another dedicated to the open spaces, exploration and travel. In fact, travel and hunting was really all that Baker – born in 1821 and the same age as Burton – ever did after inheriting a fortune from a maternal grandfather with plantations and slaves in Jamaica. Married in his teens, Baker lived abroad, briefly managing a plantation in Mauritius and then founding an agricultural settlement in Ceylon where he was best remembered as the man who shot more elephants than anyone else. His pedigree was also rooted in the aristocracy, an ancestor having served as Chancellor of the Exchequer to Henry VIII. When his wife died suddenly in 1855 leaving him with four children, Baker at 34 could have had the pick of

Victorian society. Instead, his children were sent to be raised by a sister, allowing him to travel and invent a powerful shotgun for killing elephants in Africa when he got there. Confident and rich, the inner man was, however, a frustrated explorer, and hearing of Speke's latest plan to explore for the Nile source Baker was envious of the challenge and the potential rewards. When his great wealth failed to buy a place on Livingstone's Zambesi Expedition, he returned to the only occupation he had ever enjoyed – hunting – as mentor to the youthful Maharajah Duleep Singh of the Punjab. The search for wild boar took them up the Danube through the Iron Gates gorge to Transylvania in the Balkans, and from there across the river into the Ottoman Empire and a slave market. The Indian was astonished to see white children being bought and sold. Baker was also transfixed by a bidding war between some Turks for a young, frail slave girl with golden hair. According to some accounts she was barely fourteen. Baker always said 17. How she became a slave is not clear. Most of the white female slaves came from Balkan countries torn apart by the wars that so often engulfed the region. Whether it was compassion or passion but Baker bought the child, reputedly seized by Armenians in Transylvania. Florenz Barbara Maria Sass was Armenian, the only member of her family to survive a raid by Albanian militia. Baker renamed her Florence and took her first as a mistress, later his wife. Despite the great difference in their ages, the couple became inseparable, she eternally grateful to the man who freed her from a living nightmare. The more romantic version of their first meeting is that a Turk was successful in buying the white girl for his harem, but Baker after bribing some attendants fled with Florence to Budapest. At the time he was 38, a widower and father of four. Probably on account of her past Florence was never received at court by Queen Victoria even though Baker was knighted for services to African exploration and for naming Albert Nyanza in memory of Victoria's consort, Prince Albert of Saxe-Coburg and Gotha.

The couple returned to Central Africa in 1869 when Baker was appointed by the Egyptian Viceroy Ismail Pasha to lead a military expedition to suppress slavery and develop commerce in the White Nile region. Baker remained there as Governor General for the next four years, establishing a form of administration in the new territory he christened 'Equatoria' for his successor Colonel Charles George Gordon to build upon until this Egyptian outpost ceased to exist following the Mahdist revolt.

SELECTED CORRESPONDENCE

Agreement between Consul Petherick and the Royal Geographical Society, 4 February 1861

1. Consul Petherick undertakes, in consideration of the receipt of £1,000 towards the Expedition up the Nile to place two well-armed boats, during November, 1861, at Gondokoro, with a sufficient stock of grain to ensure to Captain Speke and his party the means of subsistence upon their arrival at that place.
2. If Captain Speke shall not arrive in November, 1861, that Consul Petherick shall proceed with an armed party southwards towards Lake Nyanza to meet him.
3. If Captain Speke shall arrive at Gondokoro before June, 1862, Consul Petherick promises to assist Captain Speke in making any explorations which Captain Speke may deem desirable.
4. It being further understood that in the event of Captain Speke not having arrived by that time at Gondokoro, Consul Petherick shall not be bound to remain beyond June, 1862.

Instructions for Consul Petherick's proposed Expedition up the White Nile in aid of Captains Speke and Grant, Feb. 8, 1861

THE President and Council of the Royal Geographical Society having ascertained that the amount of subscriptions will not be sufficient to enable you to remain two years to the southward of Gondokoro, and thus to carry out your proposition in full, proceed now to give you instructions whereby the great object of their desire – the rendering assistance to the expedition under Captains Speke and Grant – can best be accomplished with the means at their disposal. By leaving England in March, you will be enabled to reach Khartoum in time to equip two boats with a supply of provisions sufficient for your own and Captain Speke's party until June, 1862. With these you will proceed to Gondokoro, where it is very desirable you should arrive early in the month of October, that is to say, as soon as possible after the cessation of the rains. You will then, in the event of Captain Speke not having arrived, leave a trust-worthy person with a sufficient force in charge of the boats, the maintenance of these until June, 1862 at Gondokoro, being of primary importance. The next object the President and

Council have in view is, that you should proceed in the direction of Lake Nyanza, with a view of succouring Captain Speke, and bringing him and his party in safety to the depot at Gondokoro. The President and Council do not attempt to lay down any limit to this exploration, but, fully trusting in your known zeal and energy, feel assured that you will do all in your power to affect the above-mentioned object, without serious risk to the lives of the party under your command. Should the junction with Captain Speke be secured, which there is every reason to believe it will be, previous to June, 1862, you will consult with him as to the best means of employing the period which will elapse before the change of the monsoon will permit you to descend the Nile, in extending our knowledge of the adjoining region. In entrusting you with the sum which has been subscribed for this purpose the President and Council, considering themselves accountable to the subscribers for its proper expenditure, will require an account of its disbursement. If circumstances should prevent your meeting with Captain Speke's expedition they consider that you are entirely relieved from the responsibility of remaining, yourself or detaining the boats longer than June, 1862 at Gondokoro. The President and Council desire to impress upon you the necessity of obtaining as frequently as possible astronomical observations for the ascertainment of your geographical position, and that you forward, as often as opportunity offers, copies of your journal to the Secretary of this Society. A list of instruments, together with instructions respecting their use, and notices of such phenomena as it is likely you will have an opportunity of observing, is herewith appended, to which also are added manuals on Ethnology, Botany, and Zoology to each of which sciences as well as Geology you will have an opportunity of adding much new information. In addition to the 'Hints for Travellers', published by this Society, particular instructions relative to the peculiar character of the great river you are about to explore have been prepared, and which, it is to be hoped, will assist you in making observations which will throw much light on the geography of this region. The President and Council take this opportunity of expressing their admiration of the spirit of enterprise which has induced you at great personal risk and possibly considerable pecuniary loss, to undertake the charge of this expedition and they hope, under God's providence, you may not only succeed in affording succour to the Zanzibar Expedition at a period when it will be most in need of it, but that you will succeed in opening a new field to the civilizing influences of commerce.

List of instruments, books supplied to Consul Petherick by the Society: Quintant by Cary; sextant by Casella; telescope, with tripod stand, by Troughton and Simms; prismatic compass by Troughton and Simms; artificial horizon by Troughton and Simms; mathematical instruments and pocket-case by Cary; boiling-water apparatus, complete, by Casella; chronometer by Barraud and Lund; parallel ruler (12-inch) by Cary; protractor (6-inch), ivory, by Cary; Raper's Navigation; Nautical Almanacs, 1861–2; forms and field books for recording latitude, meridian, and circumference; and timepieces.

The exchange of correspondence between Petherick and the Royal Geographical Society began the moment he returned to Britain. The last two letters clearly state their respective positions:

Petherick to H. W. Bates, Assistant Secretary, the Royal Geographical Society, 23 June 1865:

Sir,
With reference to the Memorandum communicated to me on the 17th instant, permit me to express great surprise at the very limited view the Committee has therein taken of the extent of my exertions to relieve the Speke Expedition. By reference to the documents alluded to, it will appear that for reasons therein assigned, in order to hope for a successful result, an expedition on a much larger scale than the one agreed to had become indispensable; therefore, during the greater part of the time originally contemplated for its duration, instead of two, I had *seven* boats employed for the relief of Captains Speke and his party.

One of these boats laden with stores of various descriptions reached Gondokoro against unprecedented difficulties in October 1862, and, according to instructions, it remained there until the arrival of Captains Speke and Grant, from which they drew a certain amount of stores and grain, which Mr Baker had it not in his power to supply.

Another expedition of three boats left Khartoum in December 1862, and arrived at Gondokoro in January 1863, prior to Mr Baker. One of these (the Kathleen) had been taken possession of by Captain Speke, a portion of whose effects were on board on my arrival at Gondokoro.

The expedition from my trading station southwards, I beg to say, was an *exploring and not a trading one*; and notwithstanding the return of two boats under the charge of Abd il Majid in disobedience to my orders, on the 10th of May 1862, from Gondokoro, and seven weeks prior to the date fixed for the termination of my agreement, it took place consequent on the certain information conveyed to him by a person in charge of de Bono's station, of the impossibility of Captain Speke reaching Gondokoro before the following season.

Again permit me to state, the slaves discovered by me in the possession of Abdd il Majid, were not brought by him from my station, but were in conjunction with other traders, carried off from the vicinity of Gondokoro.

Upon a reconsideration of the question, I feel the Committee will give me credit for continuing my exertions beyond the allotted time as expressed in the agreement, but in full accordance with the interpretation of the real views of the Council of the Royal Geographical Society as conveyed to me in their instructions for my guidance. Captain Speke not having been able to keep time, and the object in view being his relief, the continuation of my efforts to attain that end must at the time have met with the approval of the Society, insomuch as, on the report of my death, its wishes are distinctly recorded by a Minute of the Council dated January 26th 1863, and to which, for a just appreciation of my efforts, permit me respectfully to refer the Committee.

The Society wasted no time in replying, the Assistant Secretary Bates informing Petherick it did not consider he merited any special recognition for his efforts. Furthermore, it repeated its assertion that he had failed to have a boat waiting for the Speke Expedition throughout the period stipulated in the agreement. Consequently, the Minute entered in its records stated:

MINUTE OF COUNCIL

In June 1860, Mr Consul Petherick, then about to revisit the White Nile for the purpose of trade, suggested that his expedition might render important service to Captains Speke and Grant, if the Royal Geographical Society were please to avail themselves of the opportunity. He represented that Gondokoro was deserted by traders, even by natives, for part of the time between November and June and that Captain Speke's party would risk starvation if they arrived during that interval. After that, the only practicable route to Khartoum lay by river, and the boats were not to be procured at Gondokoro except by chance from the ivory traders. Lastly, that Captains Speke and Grant would find themselves in serious difficulties if unsupported by persons who were familiar with the language and customs of the northern tribes. The good-will of many Fellows of the Society, as evinced by voluntary contributions, to which the Council contributed £100 on the part of the Society, finally took the shape of an Agreement (see Appendix) between the Royal Geographical Society and Mr Petherick. A sum of £1,000 was placed in his hands, and he engaged, on his part, to station as a depot two well-armed, provisioned boats at Gondokoro, in November 1861, with a supply of provisions sufficient for his own and Captain Speke's party until June 1862, 'the maintenance of these until June 1862 at Gondokoro being of primary importance.' (Instructions, 'Proceedings,' Vol. XL). Also Mr Petherick undertook, in the event of the non-arrival of Captain Speke, to go southwards as far as he could, to endeavour to meet and succour him.

Lastly, Mr Petherick was entirely relieved from the responsibility of remaining himself or detaining the boats longer than the end of June 1862.

In considering how far Mr Consul Petherick has fulfilled his engagement to the Society, it is proper to make allowances for the disasters which befell him when engaged in his own trading pursuits, and rendered him incapable of reaching Gondokoro till many months after the latest of the above dates. Difficulties of transport in Egypt, partly due to the absence of camels at Korosko, delayed Mr Petherick's arrival at Khartoum till November 1861, at which date he had undertaken that the boats should have been stationed at Gondokoro. However, immediately on his arrival at Khartoum he dispatched two boats, which reached Gondokoro in January 1862.

A misconception now appears to have risen on the part of the Egyptian under whose charge they were. Instead of maintaining the two boats until the end of June 1862, with stores to await Captain Speke's arrival, the Egyptian proceeded westward, six or eight days journey from the White Nile, to a trading station belonging to Mr Petherick. Thence he dispatched an agent southwards, in order Mr Petherick states, in search of Captain Speke's party, and carrying letters for him; but as they did not follow the course of the river, they were not travelling in the direction from which expedition might have been expected to arrive.

Stores were bartered on Mr Petherick's account and the Egyptian captured slaves on his own. He then sailed back from Gondokoro from Khartoum early in May, and met Mr Petherick, who, discovering the slaves, sent the Egyptian in irons to Khartoum. Mr Petherick ordered back one of the boats to Gondokoro: he himself travelling overland did not reach that place till February 1863, four days after Captain Speke's arrival, and ten months after the termination of the agreement with the Royal Geographical Society.

The boat Mr Petherick had ordered back to Gondokoro was stationed there when Captains Speke and Grant arrived; but, according to the statement of Captain Speke, the agent in charge of her made no offer whatever to assist them gratuitously with provisions. They bought certain articles as any other customers might have done, at the store belonging to Mr Petherick, which was established like that of other traders at Gondokoro; but nothing whatever was offered by Mr Petherick's men, who seemed entirely occupied on their master's business. They were wholly silent as to any orders having been given by Mr Petherick to afford succour to the travellers; and they gave no letters, nor did they bring any other communication to them.

It was through Mr Baker that Captains Speke and Grant became aware that a subscription of £1,000 had been raised in England at Mr Petherick's solicitation, and placed in his hands for the purpose of establishing a depot to relieve them on their arrival at Gondokoro.

The Council are of the opinion from these facts that Mr Petherick complied with his agreement with the Society to keep boats at Gondokoro between November 1861 and June 1862, *to the extent only of having provisioned boats at that place with communications for the travellers between the months of January and May 1862* [author's italics].

The Council are satisfied that he used considerable exertion in endeavouring to recover the time he had unhappily lost between Alexandria and Khartoum. They are also aware that his efforts were the more praiseworthy on account of the difficulties due to an exceptionally early change in the monsoon, and to unusual floods on the river, and also on account of the existing disturbances among the populations of the White Nile.

Mr Petherick's proposal to search in his own person for the travellers had no result owing to the above-mentioned causes of delay on his journey. The expedition under the charge of his agent seems to have been little more than a private trading journey, and that in a direction in which the travellers were not likely to be found.

With regard to Mr Petherick's enterprises after June 1862, the date at which his agreement with the Society had come to an end, *the Council do not consider that any special recognition is due from the Society to Mr Petherick. They are unable to satisfy themselves that Mr Petherick's proceedings after that date were seriously modified by any other motives than his own private speculations in trade* [author's italics].

Select Bibliography

Baker, Samuel, 'Diaries', National Library of Scotland.

Baker, Samuel, *Albert N'yanza, Great Basin of the Nile* (The Echo Library, 2005).

Beachey, R. W., 'The East African Ivory Trade in the Nineteenth Century', *Journal of African History*, VIII, 2 (1967).

Blackwood, William, 'The death of Speke', *Blackwood's Magazine*, October 1864.

'Blue Books,'Commissioners of Inquiry into the state of education in Wales, Part II, Brecknock, Cardigan, Radnor and Monmouth, 1847, Law Library, Cardiff University.

Bradnum, Frederick, *The long walks: journeys to the sources of the White Nile* (London: 1969, 1970).

Burton, Richard Francis, *First footsteps in East Africa* (London: Longman, Brown, Green, and Longmans, 1856).

Burton, Richard Francis, *The lake regions of Central Africa* (London: Tinsley, 1860).

Burton, Richard Francis, *The Nile basin, Part I. Showing Tanganyika to be Ptolemy's western lake reservoir* [by Burton]; Part II. *Captain Speke's discovery of the source of the Nile* [by James McQueen], London, 1864.

Carnochan, W. B., *The sad story of Burton, Speke, and the Nile, or was John Hanning Speke a cad?* (Stanford University: 2006).

Chartist Archives, Newport Public Library.

Cumming, Duncan, *The Gentleman Savage* (London: Century Hutchinson, 1987).

Fabian, Johannes, *Out of our minds, Reason and Madness in the Exploration of Central Africa* (Berkeley: University of California Press, 2000).

Farr, William, 'Statistics of the Civil Service of England with observations on the constitution of funds to provide for fatherless children and widows', *Journal of the Royal Statistical Society of London*, 12 (1849).

Gray, Richard, *A History of the Southern Sudan, 1839–1889* (Oxford University Press: 1961)

Hall, Richard, *Lovers on the Nile* (London: William Collins, 1980).

Hansal, M, *Neuste Briefe aus Chartum in Central Africa* (Vienna: 1855).

Harrison, William, *Burton and Speke* (New York: 1982).

Harrison, William, *Mountains of the Moon* (New York: 1990).

Heuglion's, Th. V., 'Inner-Afrika, 1861/1862, V11, Berichte … uber den Agypt'.

James, Charles Herbert, *What I remember about myself and old Merthyr* (1889).

Kenrick, G. S., 'Varteg Ironworks', lecture, Pontypool Mechanics Institute, 1840.

Maitland, Alexander, *Speke* (London: 1971).

Holroyd, Richard, 'Notes on a Journey to Kordofan in 1836–37', *Journal of the Royal Geographical Society*, vol. IX, Part 2.

Johnston, Harry Hamilton, *The Nile Quest* (London: 1903).

Lecky, W. E., *History of European morals from Augustus to Charlemagne* (1869).

Loftus, Ernest Achey, *Speke and the Nile sources* (London: 1954).

Moorehead, Alan, *The White Nile* (London: 1960).

Murdoch, Sophia [née Speke], *Records of the Speke family* (1922), privately printed.

National Library of Scotland, *James Augustus Grant, 1827–1892: African explorer and illustrator* (Edinburgh: NLS, 1982).

National Library of Scotland, *Papers of James Augustus Grant (1827–92) and John Hanning Speke (1827–64)* (Marlborough: 2003).

Pallme, Ignatius, *Travels in Kordofan* (London: J. Madden and Co., 1844).

Petherick, John, *Egypt, the Soudan and Central Africa, with explorations from Khartoum on the White Nile to the regions of the equator* (London: Tinsley, 1861).

Petherick, John and Katherine, *Travels in Central Africa* (Tinsley, London 1869), 2 vols.

Ruppell, Eduard, *Reizen in Nubien Kordofan und dem Petraischen Arabien Vorzuglich in Geograpghisch Statistischen Hinsicht* (Frankfurt am Main: 1829).

Russegger, Joseph, *Riesen in Europa, Asien und Afrika*, vol. 3.

Santi, P., and Hill, R., *The Europeans in the Sudan 1834–1878* (Oxford: Clarendon Press, 1880).

Sforza, G., ed., *Un Lucchese in Africa, lettere di Adolfo Antognoli* (Lucca: 1878).

Spaulding, Jay, 'Slavery, Land Tenure and Social Class in the Northern Turkish Sudan 1820–1881', *International Journal of African Historical Studies 15*, 1(1982).

'Sudan', (*Petermann's Mith., Erganz* 11: 1862).

Speke, John Hanning, *The Discovery of the Source of the Nile* (Edinburgh: William Blackwood, 1863).

Speke, John Hanning, *What led to the discovery of the source of the Nile* (William Blackwood, Edinburgh: 1864)

Speke, John Hanning, 'Captain Speke's adventures in Somali Land', *Blackwood's Magazine* 87, 1860.

Speke, John Hanning, 'Journal of a cruise on the Tanganyika lake and discovery of the Victoria Nyanza lake', *Blackwood's Magazine* 86, 1859.

Speke, John Hanning, 'Discovery of the Victoria Nyanza', *Adventure and Sport* 1, 1859.

Speke, John Hanning, '*My second expedition to eastern inter-tropical Africa*' (Cape Town: 1860, privately printed).

Speke, John Hanning, 'Captain Speke's discoveries in Central Africa', *Cape Monthly* 7, 1860.

Thomas, H. B., 'Giovanni Miani and the White Nile', *Uganda Journal* 6, 1942.

Yeo, Eileen Yeo, and Thompson, E. P., eds, *The Unknown Mayhew* (London 1971).

Wauvermans. H., ed., 'Pruyssenaere, letters to his parents and others', *Bull. Soc. Roy. Géogr. D'Anvers*, xix (1930).

Wilkins, Charles, *The History of the Iron, Steel, Tinplate and Other Trades of Wales* (1903).

Index

Abil il-Majid 83, 90; carries slaves on Petherick boat 92; his defence, 93, 138
Albert Nyanza 75; Baker Expedition 115; discovery 120–1
Antognoli, Adolfo 40, 59
Antinori, Marquis 81
Azande 34, 68, 99

Baker, Sir Samuel, born, xi, 37; on slavery 38, 87; pursues the Pethericks up the Nile 84–9; allegations against Petherick 102; poisons Speke's mind 104; welcomes Speke at Gondokoro 107; expedition to Albert Nyanza 115; confronts Kamrasi, 120–1; also Appendices 161–1
Baker, Lady Florence in Transylvanian slave market, 86, 87
Bastinado 21; and Petherick 122
Baggara Arabs 30, 49–50
Bahr al-Ghazal 36, 51, 61, 68, 81, 116
Bari 103

Bedouins 22, 23–4, 25–6
'Black Domain' 5–6
Breslau University 6–7, 9
British Anti-Slavery Society 12; and Times 31
Browne, William 34
Brownell, James dies, 95
Brun-Rollet, Antoine 33, 56, 59
Burckhardt, John Lewis 18
Burton, Sir Richard Francis, born, xi, 3, 47–8, 63–4; case against Speke 114; criticism of Foreign Office 124; supports Petherick 124–5; at RGS Bath Conference 127, 128, 129; also Appendices 161

Castle Hotel 7–8
Colquhoun, Richard (Consul General) 76–7; advises Foreign Secretary 112; clears Petherick 137
Crawshay, William 5, 7
Codex Sinaiticus 23

Darwin, Charles in Wales, 10
De Malzac, Alphonse 33, 54, 61; dies of syphilis 104; slaves 141

De Bono, Andrea 33, 43
De Bono, Amabile (also Muso) 33,
    91; transporting slaves 93;
    razzia 94; and Petherick 103
Dinkas 34, 68; slaves 89
Djour 56–7

Eastern Desert 12, 25
El Obeid 12; and slavery, 27–8
El Fashar (Darfur) 34–6

Falaro 103
Falls, Major 8
Felkiu, E. W. (Dr) 46–7
Felucca 14, 14
Foreman, William (Billy Ready
    Money Money) 5, 9
Foxcroft 75

Galton, Francis (Secretary RGS),
    on native Africans, 143–4
Gondokoro 49, 56, 73; Catholic
    mission closes 84, 104; the
    'perfect hell' 106–7, 114
Grant, James Augustus 72; 'where's
    Petherick' 108; also
    Appendices 160–1
Guest, Josiah 7
Gum Arabic 24, 28

Hartz Mountains 10
'Hermit of Mountain Ash' 7
Holroyd, Richard and slavery,
    29–30
Hornby, Sir Edmund 94–5, 142

Ivory 39–40, 52

Kaka 50, 89
Kamrasi 120

Kathleen 75, 77, 79; passes slave
    caravan 81, 83, 102, 104, 107,
    108; dinner aboard for Speke,
    Grant, Baker, 109, 11; search
    for 118, 121, 135
Khartoum 37; at Consulate 81–4
Kordofan 12, 27
Korosko 78
Kurshid Aga 94, 104, 105, 107
Kyt Island 51

Lady of the Nile 81, 84; rammed
    89; sinking 95–6, 101, 102
Lake No 51
Lewis, Richard (Dic Penderyn)
    7, 9
Lewis, Lewis (Lewsyn yr Heliwr) 7,
    8, 9
Livingstone, David 12–13, 64;
    rejects Baker 86, 129

McQueen, James support for
    Petherick, 125
McQuie, Peter 71; letter to *Times*
    125–6, 130
Melly, G. 80
Merthyr Guardian 6, 9
Merthyr Rising 7–9
Miani, Giovanni, inscription on
    tree near Equator, 78–9
Morganwg, Iolo 6
Muhammad Wad-el-Mek 103
Murray, Sir Charles (Consul
    General) 32; recommends
    Petherick as Vice-Consul in
    Sudan 32–3; 49
Muhammad Ali Pasha and Wales
    10; and slavery 12–13; and
    Mamluks 15–16; the citadel
    16; as a modernizer 16